Praise for
The Lure of Saints

"An informational yet personal account of the transformative power of the Catholic and Orthodox churches' special role models. Sweeney, in very accessible concepts and language, presents a marvelously contemporary and inclusive theology of sanctity and saints.... [B]oth a miniature encyclopedia on saints and a book of spiritual reflection." —*Catholic Library World*

"[Sweeney's] book walks non-Catholics through the notion of seeing saints as prayer partners and understanding how saints are canonized.... In the end, he believes Catholics allow for the kind of spiritual mystery that, at times, better matches life experiences." —*The Dallas Morning News*

"A compelling, instructive addition to the library of any Christian seeking companionship and wisdom on the pilgrimage toward holiness." —*Spirit & Life*

"There is a satisfying blend of the concrete (prayers, a list of feast days, 10 steps to living like a saint) with Sweeney's personal observations and historical information." —*Publishers Weekly*

"Jon Sweeney is a fine, informative writer. He has a way of discussing a variety of religious matters in clear, common sense terms.... Highly recommended." —*Church and Synagogue Library Association*

"This compelling guide includes profiles of ancient, medieval, and modern figures representing East and West; the sublime and the unusual, with special chapters exploring differences between the Catholic and Protestant imaginations." —*Spiritual Life*

Jon M. Sweeney is the author of *Strange Heaven: The Virgin Mary as Woman, Mother, Disciple, and Advocate, The St. Francis Prayer Book,* and *Born Again and Again,* a memoir that was named one of the "Best Books of 2005" by *Spirituality & Health* magazine, and given an Award of Merit by *Christianity Today.* He is also the editor of Paul Sabatier's classic biography of St. Francis, *The Road to Assisi,* which was a selection of the History Book Club, Crossings Book Club, and Book-of-the-Month Club. Jon lives with his wife and two children in Vermont.

Learn more about Jon M. Sweeney at
www.paracletepress.com/authors/sweeney

THE LURE OF
SAINTS

A Protestant Experience of Catholic Tradition

JON M. SWEENEY

PARACLETE PRESS
BREWSTER, MASSACHUSETTS

The Lure of Saints

2006 First Paperback Printing
2005 First Hardcover Printing

Copyright © 2005 by Jon M. Sweeney

ISBN: 1-55725-506-7

Scripture quotations are taken from the New Revised Standard
Version of the Bible, © 1989, Division of Christian Education of the
National Council of the Churches of Christ in the U.S.A. All rights
reserved. Used by permission.

Library of Congress Cataloging-in-Publication Data

The lure of saints : a Protestant experience of Catholic tradition / Jon
M. Sweeney.
  p. cm.
Includes bibliographical references and indexes.
ISBN 1-55725-506-7
1. Christian saints. 2. Christian saints—Cult. 3. Christian life—
Anglican authors. I. Title.
BX2325.S94 2005
235'.2—dc22   2005003977

10 9 8 7 6 5 4 3 2 1

Published by Paraclete Press
Brewster, Massachusetts
www.paracletepress.com

Printed in the United States of America

To the monks of
Our Lady of the Holy Spirit,
CONYERS, GEORGIA,
and
Weston Priory,
WESTON, VERMONT,
great teachers and friends.

CONTENTS

FOUR
Reality and Practice

Spiritual Practices Related to the Saints:

Preface

I CONFESS THAT I FEEL A BIT LIKE DON QUIXOTE, who read hundreds of books on chivalry and knighthood and then foolishly determined to wander the world imitating knights by righting wrongs, helping ladies in distress, and bringing nobility back to the people along his path. Quixote often scolded Sancho Panza, his infinitely cleverer companion, for laughing at his expense, talking too much, and questioning his actions. A wickedly funny character created by Miguel de Cervantes for his famous novel by the same name, Don Quixote is perhaps the greatest idealist in history, fictional or true. He is at times a holy fool, a saint (according to W. H. Auden), and a mirror image of each person who tries hard to be something he or she has read about in books.

Don Quixote is considered foolish precisely because he wholeheartedly believes that what he has read in books about medieval knights actually happened. He is egotistical because he sincerely believes that he, too, can be a gallant knight. But irony is rich throughout the novel, as we are never quite sure if Don Quixote might actually be the sanest person around. He never seems to know that he is playing a role, as in a play—because a knight is very clearly not what Don Quixote is, deep down, with all of his bumbling and mistakes. Perhaps such role-playing is what we all are doing, at least those of us who are trying to imitate the explorers and exemplars who have gone before us. This book is written with the overriding convictions that the stories of the saints are actually stories of God at work in the world in and through us, that the truth of Christianity can be known only in imitation of Christ and those faithful who have gone before us, and that to try to be a saint is definitely a role worth playing.

Introduction

IT IS NO ACCIDENT THAT OUR IMAGES OF FAMOUS SAINTS, of Christ, even of God the Father tend to resemble us. God as the friendly, bearded old man in the clouds is ever present not just in ancient and medieval icons but in today's Sunday school leaflets. Scandinavians have produced many a Christ with blond hair and fair skin, and Italian Renaissance painters usually created images of Jesus that looked a lot like Italians. Late medieval artists painted crusader armor on St. George and others who could symbolize and support the wars brought on by the West. More recently, artists who stand in the liberation theology tradition have depicted Jesus and popular saints like Francis of Assisi as liberators of the poor and oppressed. Fund-raising ads for Catholic missions in northern Alaska (Diocese of Fairbanks) often feature a modern icon of the Madonna and Child modeled after <u>Inuits</u>. Less reverently, one young digital-collage artist recently depicted the popular Virgin of Guadalupe in a floral-patterned bikini, complete with bare midriff. It was displayed at the Museum of International Folk Art in Santa Fe, New Mexico, and created quite a stir, but in truth, it may resemble the majority of us most of all.

In many ways, beyond the work of artists, we cannot see the divine apart from ourselves. Indeed, we are not supposed to—or, at least, not yet. Saints are first and foremost the people of God—all people, alive or dead, who are graced by the Spirit of God. No wonder we see ourselves reflected in them. We *are* saints! But when we talk about *the* saints we usually mean something more closely defined; we mean the exemplary figures, the important models of sanctity, who have defined over the centuries what it means to be Christian.

Saints did not originate with Christianity. Other religious traditions before Christ revered individuals, viewed them as images of the divine, and regarded them as intermediaries between believers and God. First-century Judaism, although careful to avoid idolatry in all forms, also held up biblical heroes for the faithful to emulate. Roman mythology, which filled the air during the time of Christ and the first few centuries of the church, is replete with saints, gods, and festivals throughout the year for honoring them. Many of the minor Roman deities, such as Jupiter, Mars, and Mercury, were revered and prayed to for special blessings, just as Christian saints became patrons of particular causes and professions. The bones of the dead were often deposited in special burial grounds, and prayers were offered to various spirits of the dead. Archaeologists have discovered that rural villas as well as urban homes in the Roman Empire had a room set aside as a shrine to a specific patron deity, similar to the domestic shrines to patron saints that became popular in Christian homes several centuries later. The vestal virgins of Roman religion were chosen from the best families and installed as attendants at the temple of Vesta in the Forum. These girls had real duties, such as guarding the sacred fire in the temple and ensuring that it never went out, but they also were endowed with special powers that are similar to those later supposed to be possessed by the Christian saints. A criminal on death row would be pardoned, for instance, if his gaze met that of one of the vestal virgins. They were like saints in the perceived sanctity that their very physical presence created.

The Romans did not exclude foreign gods or goddesses from the pantheon of accepted deities, either. Many Greek gods were reverenced side by side in harmony with their Roman counterparts. Both the Egyptian Isis and the Persian Mithras had a devoted following and a widely popular cult. It was not until the emperor Constantine I, a converted Christian, ruled in the early fourth century that these old practices fell away and were replaced by many devotions to the saints and other Christian devotions.

The church may have inherited some of its ideas about saints from earlier religions, but this sort of borrowing and adoption has always been common. Consider, for instance, how Christianity grew from Judaism. We understand who Jesus was and is in light of how the first Christians, who were Jewish, borrowed from and interpreted the Hebrew Scriptures. When the apostle Paul compared Jesus to the Passover lamb that had been slain centuries earlier, the metaphor stood for faith in Jesus as a renewal and fulfillment of ancient Judaism. We grafted our faith onto the root of the covenant between God and Abraham, Isaac, and Jacob.

Or consider Christmas. It was not until the mid-fourth century that December 25 was officially declared the day of the Nativity. Most scholars argue that Jesus most likely was born in Bethlehem in the springtime, because the shepherds would have tended their flocks in springtime. When the fourth-century pope announced this change he was consciously offering a spiritual antidote to a pagan holiday. Parties around the winter solstice were popular in ancient Rome, and Christmas offered Christians an opportunity to party for a better cause. We should not reject the tradition of saints in the church simply because we did not come up with the idea first.

When we contemplate saints, we are really thinking about ourselves. Their lives reflect what we wish for, what we desire most deeply, and the direction in which we are headed in life. Saints can be mirrors for us, but when we feel separated from God, they can be barriers as well.

To painters, saints make good subjects, as they tell stories with symbolism. Painters surround the saints they depict with objects of meaning from their lives, and particularly in the first fifteen centuries of Christianity, when stories and traditions were passed down by word of mouth. The simple expression on the face of a saint and the setting of the picture could have significant meaning. Even the uneducated peasant of the Middle

Jesus' birth?

Ages would have associated a dog with St. Bernard of Montjoux, a wolf with St. Francis of Assisi, a pen in the hand with St. Benedict of Nursia, a monstrance with St. Clare, bees with St. Isidore of Seville, and serpents at the feet with St. Patrick. Similarly, the uneducated peasant would have understood the symbols for what they represented. For instance, St. Lucia holding human eyes in her palm stood for a woman placing love of God over love of a man.

To theologians, saints each mean something very distinct and teachable. Many of the saints were themselves theologians, and some are even known as "doctors" of the church, a sign of the great instructional value that their writings have. So far thirty-two saints have been honored as doctors in the Catholic church. This sort of celebration of theological influence is actually similar in Protestant traditions: United Methodists today remember the importance of Georgia Harkness (d. 1974); members of the Evangelical Lutheran Church in America honor Krister Stendahl; and Mennonites discuss the teachings of John Howard Yoder (d. 1997) as foundational contributions to the faith.

Theologians who have commented on the saints over the centuries have primarily emphasized the lessons of virtue to be learned from examining their lives. Children in Catholic Sunday schools learn many of these stories before they can even read. But these lessons of goodness and courage easily become static images. Like petrified forests, the saints stand mighty and firm. Seen only as heroes of virtue, though, the saints are difficult to relate to; they are little more than the plastic statues in the gift shop, or the plaster statues on the lawn.

To poets, saints are the embodiment of psychological archetypes. The combination of sin and victory over sin in their lives highlights universal themes such as desire, shame, loss, love, and ecstasy. The life of Blessed Angela of Foligno exemplifies all these universal themes at once, as does that of the more recent Padre Pio. The very human emotions of even the most famous and revered of saints are an indication that saintliness is still much closer to humanness than godliness.

Poets have also written for centuries about saintly antidotes to the world's temptations. Literature is chock-full of references to saints; some of these writings, including lovely poems by Richard Crashaw, George Herbert, and Dante, we will look at in more detail in this book. In contrast, other popular poets have written verse that makes the most sense when read as reactions to saintly piety. The English Romantics, such as Shelley and Wordsworth, with their emphasis on finding the divine in nature, not the church, and their focus on the interior life, but without Scripture or saint as a guide, fit this category. The words of religious poets about the saints often make less sense to us than do the more naturalistic phrases of the Romantics.

Painters, theologians, and poets depict, praise, and interpret the lives of saints when they see the world in a particular way—as a place where time is relative in the face of eternity, and where the saints remain among us. It is a mistake to view the saints as chosen ones who were given special access to divine mysteries. Most Christians (Protestants, in particular) have been taught to believe only when we have seen. But we all need to believe more completely, and sometimes this means that we need to train ourselves to see anew. Jonathan Edwards once said, "Saints see what everyone else sees—they just see it differently." I think he's right, and that's part of why I am drawn to them—so that I might learn to see differently, too.

Much of what is written in these pages is personal. My own experiences with the saints are my real reasons for writing, and they are offered here in the midst of my reflections and research. I don't believe it is possible to engage with the saints—or with God, for that matter—in a purely objective way. Approximating their passion, more than learning facts about them, will lead us to understand their saintliness. For this reason, too, I have invited friends and other spiritual writers and teachers to share their own very practical experiences with the saints. The spiritual practices of Sr. Rosemarie Greco, D.W.; Abbot M. Basil Pennington, O.C.S.O.; popular writer Mitch Finley; Fr. Murray Bodo, O.F.M.; Br. Wayne Teasdale; artist Marek Czarnecki; and Rev. Mary E. Haddad are offered throughout in special sections called, simply, "Practices."

Many Kinds of Catholic, Many Types of Protestant

IN EVERYDAY USAGE, THE TERM *CATHOLIC* USUALLY MEANS A person who is a member of the Roman Catholic church. But as there are some twenty autonomous churches within the Catholic church, it isn't ever that simple. As I once heard Sr. Joan Chittister explain, "This means that there are many different ways of being Catholic."[1] These churches include the Maronite, which originated in Syria and whose members speak Arabic, and the Chaldean, which began in Iraq and whose members speak a modern form of Aramaic; each of these churches in the Catholic church counts at least 50,000 members in the United States. I am an expert on none of these.

In ancient terms, *Catholic* is a spiritual identifier of a different sort. It means one who is a Christian in the broadest of all senses, a member incorporate in the universal, mystical body of Christ, without division. This was the meaning of *Catholic* before terms such as *Roman Catholic, Orthodox,* or *Protestant* came to exist. The *Oxford English Dictionary* defines *Catholic* in this sense as "Catholic Church, Church Catholic: The Church universal, the whole body of Christians." I count myself a Catholic in this broad sense.

There are three major branches growing off the trunk of the Christian family tree. The roots nourish each of them, because they all were once one. The Catholic churches, with more than a billion members, make up the largest of the three, and the Roman Catholic church is the dominant of these. Its historical roots are in Rome, the pope being the bishop of Rome. The apostle Peter is believed to have been the first pope, which is why he often holds keys to heaven in icons and religious paintings. The Orthodox churches of the East (Russian, Greek, Latvian, Serbian, and others), counting about a quarter of a billion members, make up the second branch. Sharing a common history with Catholicism up until the Great Schism of the eleventh century, the Orthodox church's historical roots are in Constantinople, the former seat of the Byzantine Empire, today's Istanbul. The various Protestant churches, with nearly half a billion members, form the third branch; these are the reforming churches that began separating from Rome in the sixteenth century. The largest of the Protestant denominations in America is Baptist (with more than fifty denominations). The Protestant denomination that most resembles the Roman Catholic church in liturgy and worldwide scope is the Anglican Communion, with its historical roots in Canterbury, England, but with its greatest growth today coming from various parts of Africa. Most Anglicans in the United States are members of the Episcopal Church.

Throughout this book I often use the catchall terms *Catholic*, *Orthodox*, and *Protestant*, as if each word has only one possible meaning. I realize the weakness of the approach, but it is necessary in order to avoid what are ultimately unnecessary subtleties in a book such as this one. There are more than 30,000 Protestant denominations throughout the world today, so generalizing about Protestants is clearly difficult but also inevitable. In many places throughout this book, I suggest what a Protestant response might be to a particular issue. In many cases, that Protestant is me; in others, it might be you.

For the sake of convenience, we will focus mostly on the relationship between Catholic practices regarding saints and the various Protestant reactions to them. It is important for Protestants to realize that Catholics are not monolithic in their beliefs. Many contemporary American Catholics, for instance, spend very little time thinking about the saints, analyzing the meaning of the sacraments, or even paying attention to the official statements that come from Rome. Their largely unexamined faith is formed partly by Catholic tradition and partly by American individualism and eclecticism.

Among Catholics who do examine their beliefs, some are traditionalists who fit Protestant expectations of what a Catholic is like: they have a high regard for Vatican authority, they value practices foreign to most Protestant experience (such as saying the rosary, making confessions, and venerating saints), and some even prefer to hear Mass in Latin with no female altar servers.

On the other hand, many thoughtful Catholics call themselves progressives or liberals. Such freethinkers have been referred to as *Commonweal Catholics*, after the influential magazine that was founded in 1924 to speak to intellectuals, activists, and reformers both within and outside the church. Notables that fit into this category include activists Daniel Berrigan, John Dear, Dorothy Day, and writers such as Hans Küng, Thomas Merton, and Joan Chittister. James O'Gara, a longtime editor of *Commonweal*, wrote in his final column before retiring in 1984: "The commitment of the 'Commonweal Catholic' was and is to a church that was open and pluralistic, not rigid and authoritarian, a church that was a visible manifestation of Jesus' presence in the world."[2]

For liberal Catholics, being Catholic is more about working toward social justice and effecting positive societal change than venerating saints, making weekly confession, and dutifully adhering to each instruction from the Vatican. They tend to admire Pope John XXIII, the convener of the Second Vatican Council (1962–65), more than Pope John Paul II, who has in many ways retreated from the theological and ecclesiastical flexibility initiated at the former pope's urging.

Some Catholics believe that the conservative leanings of the current pope are more a matter of culture and nationality than of theology. John Paul II is the first non-Italian pope since 1522, when a Dutch intellectual, Adrian Dedel, assumed the throne of Peter as Adrian VI. Adrian, who reigned for less than two years, had the same sort of culturally conservative sensibilities as Karol Wojtyla, the Polish archbishop elected to the papacy in 1978. Italian novelist Roberto Pazzi recently suggested in an Op-Ed in the *New York Times*, entitled "Why the Next Pope Needs to Be Italian," that if the next elected pope is Italian, we will see less conservative attitudes on bioethical and sexual issues, more openness to contraception as a means of fighting AIDS in Africa, and more acceptance of common-law and gay couples.[3] Referring to the Italian who was the vicar of Christ for one short month before the election of John Paul II, Pazzi concluded:

> In general, at least in the past 100 years, an Italian pope, precisely because he has been trained in a proud political school like the Vatican, guarantees a more nuanced distance from politics and a warmer pastoral mission. These are qualities that the pope who died after only 34 days, the Italian John Paul I, appeared to possess: he who left the memory of himself in his name and in the suggestive declaration that "God is the Father but is also the Mother."

Introduction

Today's broad-minded American Catholics are perhaps best represented by Garry Wills, a Pulitzer Prize-winning historian, a writer, and a professor at Northwestern University. In the introduction to the new edition of his popular book *Why I Am a Catholic*, Wills explains why he remains Catholic despite his differing opinions with the church:

> Some who have read this book still ask why I am a Catholic. They must have a stereotypical view of what Catholics are, and I do not fit it. But neither do most Catholics. By large majorities they, too, differ from the pope on such things as contraception, married priests, women priests. They do not consider themselves non-Catholics, and neither do their priests. . . .
>
> I cannot leave the church because I would consider that a sin—a sin against the three theological virtues, a sin against faith, a sin against charity, a sin against hope.
>
> It would be a sin against faith because I would be saying that if the pope is wrong the church is wrong, and I must leave it. But I do not believe that the pope is the church. I never have, and neither have most Catholics through the ages.[4]

Liberal-conservative tension in the American Catholic Church was evident during the 2004 presidential race. Senator John Kerry, the first Catholic to run for president on either the Democratic or the Republican ticket since John F. Kennedy in 1960, was outspokenly in favor of abortion rights and stem-cell research, counter to the Vatican's position. The U.S. Catholic hierarchy was in a quandary, divided as to whether to be proud of Kerry for his political success and consistent faith or rebuke him for his liberal statements. A few bishops publicly announced that Kerry would be refused Communion if he worshiped at one of their parishes, but the majority of priests and bishops were quiet, including the priest that offered Kerry Communion most Sundays in Massachusetts. Inconsistencies among the U.S. bishops also exist on other issues: it is rare to hear a rebuke of a Catholic politician who favors the death penalty, for instance, which is also a stance in direct opposition to church teaching, reiterated by the current pope. In all of this, my primary point is that it is important for Protestants to remember that not all Roman Catholics think alike.

Many of the saints who are venerated throughout the year were also of a "liberal" sort—bucking tradition on occasion and following their conscience. St. Antony of Egypt (251–356), for instance, originated what has come to be known as "desert spirituality" when, at twenty years of age, he became dissatisfied with domestic and parish life and created new ways or reinvigorated old ways of being Christian, living as a hermit for the next eighty years. In contrast to the institutional church of his day and the settled life common in cities like his native Alexandria, Antony emphasized a life of personal poverty, celibacy, and solitude and of the prayer and contemplation that such conditions make possible. We can look to Antony today for inspiration when trying to opt out of the rampant and insidious consumerism that dominates our lives.

Dorothy Day (1897–1980), the cofounder of the Catholic Worker movement, will surely be canonized one day. (Her cause was opened in 2000.) She was a single mother, had an abortion long before it was legal in this country, and lived in Hollywood for a time working as a screenwriter. After her conversion, Day became convinced of the need to dedicate her life to helping the poor and disadvantaged, the homeless and hungry, and to working toward peace. In New York City, where she lived most of her life, she noticed that Catholic churches were some of the only places where the homeless and hungry could find solace. She was not born Roman Catholic but was baptized into the church and worked tirelessly the rest of her life for these causes. She opposed American involvement in World War II when it was extremely unpopular to do so. Day once explained that she never wanted to be made a saint: "You cannot dismiss me that easily!" she declared. Day's life and message have moved people today to open their homes to those in need, often calling these places Catholic Worker houses or simply hospitality houses.

Pope John XXIII, mentioned above, may also fit in this category of saint. Known as a good shepherd of a pope, he visited not only small, local parishes, but also prisoners and patients in hospitals. He opened the Second Vatican Council by stating that he wanted to bring the church up-to-date and to "let some fresh air in." As evidence of his tremendous role in working toward Christian unity, "when he died on the evening of June 3 [1963], virtually the whole world mourned his loss. Even the Union Jack was lowered to half-staff in the bitterly divided city of Belfast."[5] We can look to him today for inspiration in mediating conflicts brought on by religious differences.

PART ONE

Love and Devotion

M Y GOOD LORD, AS YOUR SERVANT I LONG TO pray to you for my friends, but as your debtor I am held back by my sins. . . . I anxiously seek intercessors on my own behalf, how then shall I be so bold as to intercede for others? What shall I do, Lord God, what shall I do? You command me to pray for them and my love prompts me to do so, but my conscience cries out against me. . . . So I pray you, good and gracious God, for those who love me for your sake and whom I love in you. . . . Love them, Author and Giver of love, for your own sake, not for mine, and make them love you with all their heart, all their soul, and all their mind.

—St. Anselm (d. 1109), from "A Prayer for Friends"[1]

CHAPTER

1

How I Came to Love
the Saints

I BECAME AN ART MUSEUM JUNKIE TWENTY YEARS AGO AS A college student in Chicago. The Art Institute on Michigan Avenue was my primary place of wandering. I was in Bible college and had been raised in a kind of fundamentalism that dispensed with all symbols, but nevertheless, I found myself drawn only to the paintings of saints. I was both fascinated and revolted by them. The more gruesome the better: blood flowing from Christ's open wounds on the cross, Salome's satisfied expression as John the Baptist's head was separated from his body at her whim. I sat for hours and gawked. This was the Bible in an entirely new light, nothing like the more rational religion of my childhood. I was drawn to the saints, but I didn't know why. I felt the lure of their images and the stories of their lives, and the strangeness of it all seemed, somehow, terribly relevant to my life.

Julian Green, an American Catholic convert living in France, wrote: "Sometimes we do things, without thinking, that make no sense to us until much later and yet appear to have been prompted by the most alert part of our being."[1]

Since those earliest days of adulthood, I have wandered the halls of museums looking for the paintings of saints, and their legends have become important for me on many levels. Bible college and the particular faith of my childhood are now long past, and my interest in both the liveliness and the ugliness of saints and their legends grows. Traveling in Europe one summer, I thought the Mona Lisa at the Louvre was nice, but I was speechless upon seeing Giotto's frescoes of St. Francis on the walls of the upper church in the basilica in Assisi. In the National Gallery in London, I found the large, famous portraits of Henry VIII and Princess Diana to be interesting, but I went straight for Giovanni di Paolo's *Saints Fabian and Sebastian*. I could feel Sebastian's defiant look as a quiver of arrows pierced his body, and I wondered to myself: *What would I have done in his place? Would I have looked so calm, so sure that I was right?* In the Uffizi in Florence, I saw that Botticelli's remarkable *Birth of Venus* was indeed remarkable, but more interesting to me was Michelangelo's *Holy Family with the Infant John the Baptist*. *How do Mary and Joseph each model the sort of relationship with God that I want to have?* I thought.

With scenes so dramatic, it is not difficult to understand how the stories of saints can grab hold of us and repel us at the same time. Art infused with religious themes speaks to spiritual passion and experience in ways that texts cannot. Just as the oral transmitting of the lives of the early saints sustained the early church, the visual transmission of saints' lives, in art museums around the world, sustains us. Even avowed skeptics are confronted with these faces, whether they like it or not, and I often wonder how they can stand it. The grimaces, the looks of inappropriate ecstasy, and the faces of quiet contentment leave even my sympathetic self frustrated; the sweetness of the expressions, the glows from the halos, and the wounds of the stigmata used to keep me moving on to the next hall. I can only wonder what they do to someone who has no spiritual interests whatsoever.

While lingering in the churches of Paris in the 1940s, Julian Green wrote:

> I stood for a moment in a corner of the cloister wearing an
> imaginary hood and with a medieval heart beating beneath

my doublet of dark green cloth, because for a variety of reasons <u>I am nostalgic for a period</u> when I believe man still, in the deepest part of his being, possessed a peace we have lost, and the place I am talking about is one of those where that inner peace seems as naturally at home as in the pages of Thomas à Kempis.[2]

I, too, have found an inner peace and a "medieval heart." I love Green's expressions for this experience of rediscovering what ancient and medieval spirituality seems to have understood without argument. I feel more at home in the sanctuary of a great church, in the halls of a cloister, or on a simple pilgrimage than I do in the everyday places of my normal life. And I've realized that it is no accident that saints are accompanying me, and meet me, in these places I have grown to love.

I realize, however, that I may not be typical. Most people I know feel completely out of place in these religious places and situations. They want just the opposite of what I want. More in line with what the Romantic poets desired, they want to discover God in secular places. The extraordinary growth of Starbucks and other "third places,"—or places to sit and be that are neither work nor home—undoubtedly owes a lot of credit to spiritual seeking outside of organized religion. Many <u>people seek spiritual experience, and find it meaningfully, in nonthreatening, nonreligious places</u>. If you are one such person, do not think that this book is not for you: I think you will find that the practice of bringing the saints actively into your life ultimately has little to do with the church you may or may not attend.

My own faith and my discovering of the spirituality of the saints is not without serious doubts. I am still a profound skeptic, only a partial convert. As a university student in Bonn, Karl Marx often went to church with a friend in order to laugh out loud in mocking protest. I've done that, too. Sometimes it does seem more appropriate to protest religion than to engage in it. Saints are not only, or always, in churches.

MY CHILDHOOD FAITH HAD NOTHING TO DO WITH SAINTS. They were weird and also somehow exotic, from another world, another type of faith. The faith of the devout Roman Catholic—full, as it sometimes is, of pieties and emotion—was as foreign to my young, rational, Protestant worldview as were the exotic religions of India or Africa. The kind of religion that appeals to the senses was the opposite of what made sense to me.

The lens through which I was taught to see the world focused on images of the saints only long enough to denounce them as superstitious. Holographic images of Jesus hanging from taxi rearview mirrors, rosary beads and cross necklaces, Hail Marys and Glory Bes, halos in religious art, and memorized prayers uttered in times of crisis—all of these things were signs of inauthentic faith, or religion instead of faith, according to the teachings of my childhood. Nothing should stand in the way of a direct relationship with Jesus, we were taught, and saints—among many other things—were in the way.

Fundamentalist as it was, my church taught me that Catholics and Orthodox Christians were in need of salvation. Devotion to saints, and other forms of piety that evangelical Protestants often feel stand in the way of faith in Christ alone, was not only unnecessary, but also harmful. Anything saints-related was extra-biblical, post–New Testament, and dangerous, as kosher as a cheeseburger on Friday night had I grown up Jewish in Skokie rather than Protestant in Wheaton, both Chicago suburbs. Devotion to saints was meaningless superstition, we were taught, and had had a disastrous effect on the history of Christianity. Each generation leading up to the Protestant Reformation had made the same mistake of placing these superstitions—devotion to saints, praying to saints for help—in the way of simple, direct faith. And so, we believed, even such an influential man as Francis of Assisi may not have been a true Christian. This notion is almost unthinkable to me now, but it reflects how we sincerely believed. Those crazy miracles attributed to Francis seemed unbelievable, maybe even fraudulent; miracles themselves were barriers to, rather than evidence of, real faith. We would ask: "Why were his followers so devoted to him? Why didn't he take better care of himself, his health?" The extravagance of St. Francis's commitment, goodness, and sanctity did not endear him to our skeptical minds—it made his faith suspect.

6

Scott Hahn, one of the most popular Catholic authors in America today, is a convert, a former evangelical Protestant pastor. Hahn describes the first time he attended Mass at a Catholic church. His feelings were typical of many Protestant reactions to Catholic tradition: "I persuaded myself to go and see, as a sort of academic exercise, but vowing all along that I would neither kneel nor take part in idolatry."[3] (Hahn explains that the evangelical Protestant view of the Catholic Mass is that it is idolatry to consider that a priest "re-sacrifices" Christ each time, and to imagine that the offered Host is the substance of Christ himself, in the flesh.)

While saint devotion was completely foreign to my home and my closest circle of family and friends, it was not unknown in my neighborhood. The objects I saw in the family room of a Greek Orthodox girl who lived around the corner left my mouth gaping more than when she kissed me for the first time in her backyard. Icons, *sartores* with garlands of flowers about their wooden necks, candles burning as prayers unattended in their cups—these sights seemed as far from my living room as Cyprus or Sicily. We Protestants grew up in houses next door to Catholic or Orthodox friends who were named for saints, prayed to saints, and talked about saints in a way that seemed both very natural and very strange to us. I remember as a boy growing up in a suburb near Chicago, where Catholics made up the majority of the kids in my school, and poking fun at them in my ignorance for making the sign of the cross. I would mimic the motion and roll my eyes, saying, "What is that!" And when these eight-year-olds could not quickly explain why they did what they did, I knew in my ignorance that I was right to question it.

Then there were the phrases, amazingly convoluted phrases that sounded somehow religious, often salacious, and still so foreign to my ear: *sacred heart, consecrated virgins, precious blood, Miraculous Medal, mother of God.* I was in downtown Manila one afternoon when I first encountered the words *MOTHER OF GOD, PRAY FOR US,* written in enormous block letters on the side of a building. I was eighteen, and I had traveled to Southeast Asia as a missionary under the auspices of the Conservative Baptist Foreign Missionary Society. I had been sent as an assistant church planter to a country where more than ninety-five percent of the people called themselves Catholic. I had been sent to convert Catholics into Baptists.

This was 1986, just after the "People's Revolution" had ousted Ferdinand and Imelda Marcos from power. I paused on the street, staring up at those baffling words, thinking, *What in the world does that mean? How could God have a mother? Not possible,* I thought. A testimony to successful indoctrination is the inability we sometimes have to imagine a broader world even when it stares us in the face.

I suspect that my bewilderment on the street in Manila was and is typical of many Protestant Christians today. The world of the Catholic imagination is different from the world of Protestantism. So much divides the two ways that we see the world, describe it, and locate ourselves within it. In many ways, this book is my attempt to live in that rich Catholic world that is the heritage of all of us who live as Christians, even though I am only just beginning to see it. We who pride ourselves on reforming the church and replacing superstition with greater emphasis on preaching, teaching, and understanding the Word of God might learn something more about the spiritual life and about ourselves if we would take a fresh look at Catholic devotion.

IN THE YEARS SINCE MY GORY AND EYE-OPENING introduction to the Catholic church's heroes, I have spent thousands of hours reading about saints, talking and writing about them, making my own prayers to saints, and searching the Bible and Christian tradition for what it means to be a saint—in the past and today. I have written and edited two books about St. Francis of Assisi, the saint to whom I feel the greatest connection. No longer fundamentalist but still Protestant, I have learned that saints are for everybody. They show faith in an entirely new light, one that seems to have little connection to the cold, rational beam of my childhood religion.

All Christians share ancient traditions of making saints and practicing faith in the midst of a cloud of witnesses. Whether we are Catholic, Orthodox, or Protestant, we have inherited the saints of the first millennium of our faith. And each tradition has its own saints as well.

I invite you to join me as I explore the world of saints. In the chapters that follow, you will find many profiles of ancient, medieval, and modern figures representing both East and West, the sublime and the unusual. Special chapters explore differences between the Catholic and the Protestant imaginations, how saints were made in the past and how they are today, the radical triumph of the Protestant idea, ancient practices of relating to saints, and miracles, apparitions, and other strange, saintly behaviors.

"Why do you need all that extra stuff?" an evangelical Christian friend recently asked me when I told her about the book I was writing. She also knows of my interest and participation in other traditionally Catholic devotions. "Why isn't the grace of God enough for you?" she asked. I explained that she was talking about salvation—being sure that you've got it—and I was talking about moving on, after salvation, and finding deeper ways of building a relationship with God.

grace

Our Protestant rationalism can be misguided and over-reaching. I sometimes wonder where all our certainty comes from. Where the Catholic church is a reality unto itself—a set of traditions and beliefs and a body of believers—Protestantism, when it means that the individual conscience is more important than traditions, beliefs, and a body of believers, can become a reality only in the mind.

From the past, we can learn spiritual practices that offer us ways for head and heart to meet at last. My life in Christ involves my whole body—my emotions and my actions as well as my intellect—but I am only recently realizing this kind of faith, below my chin. That is why I love the saints: they are my guides to multifaceted faith.

I want the sort of faith that Jesus expected of Peter when he asked him to let down his nets again after Peter was tired and ready to go home: unlikely faith and, then, faith in mystery. Emily Dickinson wrote: "On subjects of which we know nothing . . . we both believe and disbelieve a hundred times an hour, which keeps believing nimble." I'd like a faith that accepts more than it rejects. I want that in my life, and I want the intimacy with God that comes of it. For the saints, the world is not a set

✓

of givens. The lives of saints are full of their open responses to God and an awareness of a world of possibilities.

I also confess that I admire Catholic pieties. Although I was taught as a child that they are blind and superstitious, my actual experience of witnessing these things firsthand, and incorporating some into my life, has taught me differently. *Piety* is a word that is out of fashion today. Much like *sentimental, piety* signals emotion gone amok, emotion at the expense of others. We Protestants don't trust it; we feel that it is excessive or manipulative. But pieties are simply practices, like daily prayer and Bible reading in Protestantism, that allow us to put our faith into practice. In the Catholic tradition, these include praying with rosary beads, making novenas (special prayers), *lectio divina* (spiritual reading), saying memorized prayers, making pilgrimages to special places, making the sign of the cross, prostrating oneself, lighting vigil candles, and many other practices related to loving Christ and knowing God's will. All these things, with the exception of *lectio*, are practices that developed in the Middle Ages primarily as ways for the average layperson, illiterate and poor but hungry of spirit, to make a spiritual connection to God and religion. Books were unavailable to most people, and liturgies were read or sung in Latin, a language unknown to all but a few. These devotions, however, became habits for people, often done without thought, and Protestants later abandoned them for that reason. But there is great value in them, and I believe that habitual devotion is not thoughtless even if it is performed without thinking.

Of course, as does anyone who is naturally skeptical, I have serious doubts about some aspects of pieties and devotions to the saints. There is no question in my mind that some practices and intentions are a lot like practicing magic, or simply asking God for favors. The communion of saints is a web of relationships that is ours to claim, to be a part of, but that doesn't imply that all ways of accomplishing this are equally good or useful. One contemporary Catholic theologian expressed the serious concerns that any good Protestant theologian might have as well:

> For many centuries the communion of saints has been structured according to the social system of patronage, taken from earth and writ large into heaven. The imagination of

this construal sees God like a monarch ruling in splendor, with hosts of courtiers ranked in descending order of importance. Being far from the throne, people need intercessors who will plead their cause and obtain spiritual and material favors that would otherwise not be forthcoming. This is put rather baldly but it is not inaccurate. Not only did the Reformation criticize this patronage structure for the way it disrupts the gospel, overshadowing Christ in whom God's gracious mercy has been poured out on the earth so that there is no need of other go-betweens; but contemporary feminist analysis also shows the pattern to be profoundly patriarchal, shaped according to a graded pyramid of power with an elite corps near the top and a male ruling figure at the point.[4]

There are compelling ways to understand our relationship, as Protestants, with the communion of saints—ways that satisfy our complaints about both abuses of power and outdated metaphors for how God works—that make sense today. That, too, is what this book is about.

Finally, I love the saints because they demonstrate God's ongoing plans for salvation: they are revealed in the lives of these ordinary-become-extraordinary people. I love the team-work of salvation. I believe that we must remove the modern invention of facing God alone, of facing the Last Judgment alone; we must remove the existential angst that we've learned from the post-Enlightenment, postmodern world. Saints—and that includes me and you—pray for one another, support one another, seek to improve one another. I want to hold up my end of the bargain, and I want to believe that you will hold up yours. Saints fertilize everything with God. We could learn something from the ways in which people in the Middle Ages spread the saints around for everyone to see, touch, understand, and know.

Who Are They, and
How Did It All Begin?

In the Beginning . . . They Had Wings

THE SAINTS OF DANTE'S *PARADISE*, THE LAST BOOK OF his famous *Divine Comedy*, are the sort of people you would never want to invite over for dinner. Each dead saint in Dante's mythology is now a star in the firmament that is paradise, a series of nine heavens. The saints sit in cocoons of light gazing forever on the Beatific Vision of the Godhead, possessing all knowledge. Each saint's place in one of these heavens of paradise is determined by how completely his or her will has been converted to the desires of God. The first apostles of Christ (minus Judas, of course) and the major figures of the Hebrew Bible and the New Testament take the top spots. There are some notable exceptions, however: Eve is not a saint in Dante's heaven.

But the places of the saints in heaven and what they do there are about as interesting as medieval discussions of how many angels may fit on the head of a pin. Who were the saints, and what did they do when they were alive?

The first saints were angels with wings, according to the chronology of the Bible. Although they may be irrelevant to us as moral guides or exemplars of virtue and holiness because of their angelic, not human, status, angel-saints are nevertheless an essential piece of Christian tradition. First among them was Michael the archangel, one of the most common saints depicted in art. Before the six days of creation, when God resided in heaven with the heavenly host, there was a very important and exalted angel by the name of Lucifer. He was so beautiful that he was known as the "Son of Morning." One day, Lucifer revolted, recruiting many other angels who no longer wished to be ruled by God. According to legend, it was Michael who then rallied the good angels against Lucifer and the other rebellious ones, literally booting them out of heaven. The book of Revelation says that Michael will once again battle Lucifer, "holding in his hand the key to the bottomless pit and a great chain" with which to bind him for 1,000 years. Frequently shown in paintings armed to the teeth and battling a demon or devil, Michael became a patron saint in times of war. Combatants prayed for his intercession and attributed victories to him. Apparitions of Michael were reported in France in the sixth and seventh centuries, including at Mont-Saint-Michel, where a famous shrine to the angelic saint still stands. Many churches are dedicated to Michael and the other two archangels mentioned in Scripture: Gabriel, the messenger of the annunciation to Mary, and Raphael, the great helper of Tobit and also possibly the angel responsible for the healing power of "the stirring of the water" at the Bethesda pool in Jerusalem (John 5:1–4). Michael is an important angel of Jewish and Muslim traditions as well as in Christianity. The ancient holiday of Michaelmas, or the Feast of St. Michael, is still celebrated in Britain on September 29 and is a bank holiday.

Lucifer was, according to some traditions, the fourth archangel and also Michael's brother before the rebellion that saw him defeated, banished from heaven, and renamed "Satan." In John Milton's epic poem, *Paradise Lost,* Raphael is sent by God to explain things to Adam after Lucifer's rebellion and to warn Adam about Lucifer's evil intent. The first two lines quoted below will remind many readers today of the Harry Potter stories, in which the wizards do not speak the name of the wizard-gone-bad, Voldemort.

Early ivory carving of St. Michael with scepter and holding the orb of earth in his trusted hand.

Satan, so call him now; his former name
Is heard no more in Heav'n; he of the first,
If not the first Archangel, great in Power,
In favor and preeminence, yet fraught
With envy against the Son of God.

Raphael goes on to explain that Lucifer initiated his rebellion when God made it clear that the Son of God was the anointed Messiah King, the second in command.

Angels reappear throughout Christian history in the lives of the saints. Visitations from angels, who are sometimes disguised as strangers or animals or birds, often punctuate turning points and crises of vocation in saints' lives, and angels appear as well to deliver divine messages. Even fallen angels appear from time to time. Brendan, the seafaring Irish saint, speaks to a bird that has landed on the prow of his boat, asking it, "Who are you, and why are all of you here?" The bird responds that it is one of the fallen angels who made the mistake of following Lucifer, now left to wander the earth singing God's praises rather than doing the same at God's feet in heaven.

Angels, as saints, are hardly relevant in our lives in the here and now. The true communion of saints is fully human, not angelic, and is trying to transform the earth, which is very different from fluttering about the heavens. As I hope will become clear over the course of this exploration, the primary importance of sainthood is that it leads to our complete humanness, to our becoming who we are in the kingdom of God.

The three most important saints to the early Christians were the Blessed Virgin Mary (we will take a closer look at her in chapter 5); Peter, the outspoken disciple of Jesus; and Paul, the convert to Christ who expanded the message to non-Jews. Both Peter and Paul were martyred in Rome before the biblical Gospels were composed, and eventually—by the time the emperor Constantine converted to Christianity in 313 CE made Rome safe for Christians—June 29 became their joint feast day. The abbreviation SS. or Sts. is used to indicate saints, plural, and throughout Rome today one can see references to SS. Peter and Paul. Ancient history tells of solemn processions around the city on June 29, from St. Peter's Basilica on Vatican Hill (where the Renaissance-era St. Peter's Basilica stands today) to St. Paul's Basilica on the Ostia road to a shrine dedicated to both saints along the Appian Way.

Early Martyrs and Heroes

THE EARLY CHRISTIANS UNDERSTOOD CERTAIN PASSAGES OF Scripture much more intimately than we do today. Imagine, for instance, how the citizens of Rome or Carthage or any large city of the Roman Empire would have heard these words from Psalm 116 during the worst decades of persecution of Christians:

> What shall I return to the LORD
> 	for all his bounty to me?
> I will lift up the cup of salvation
> 	and call on the name of the LORD,

I will pay my vows to the LORD
    in the presence of all his people.
Precious in the sight of the LORD
    is the death of his faithful ones.
O LORD, I am your servant;
    I am your servant, the child of your serving girl;
    You have loosed my bonds.
I will offer to you a thanksgiving sacrifice
    and call on the name of the LORD.
I will pay my vows to the LORD
    in the presence of all his people,
in the courts of the house of the LORD,
    in your midst, O Jerusalem.
Praise the LORD! (Psalm 116:12–19)

This Scripture sounds like a confession, a badge of honor, for the early martyrs and any loved ones left behind by those who had been sacrificed for the faith. In the late 300s CE, a half century after the worst of the persecutions, Augustine of Hippo, the great theologian and convert, remembered what the amphitheater experience was like. These words, preached to his congregation at Advent, must have been difficult to hear:

When I used to go to these games myself, I noticed that people reacted in two quite different ways.

First, there was the sensualist response—people screaming and shouting as the Christian Martyrs fell to the jaws of the jungle cats, when their heads were cleft from their shoulders, when their carcasses were tossed into the furnace!

But that bloodthirsty response in other people, under some circumstances, could and did indeed change into a spiritual one. They came to watch the games, not through bloodshot eyes but, apparently, through angelic eyes. Oh they saw the bones broken, and they watched the blood flow, and they heard the heart-rending screams of the Martyrs. But then they came to see the unseen; that's to say, the faith of the Christians as they died the death on the arena sand. There was no sight at the games quite like this! A body being mauled while its soul remained unscratched. I know. I've been there.

Now when I say these things aloud in the church, you begin to see them with your own eyes; then, you hear them with your own ears. I know, many of you've never been to the amphitheater at all—you still loathe everything that takes place there—but my words have just now brought you right there, haven't they? I can tell by your tears.[1]

That is why we love the martyrs. A verse such as Psalm 116:15 ("Precious in the sight of the LORD is the death of his faithful ones") might only remind us of extremist religious rhetoric today, but not so 2,000 years ago. The early Christian martyrs were witnesses to their convictions to the point of a horrible death. Their martyrdom had nothing to do with causing harm to others, or pitting enemies—either spiritual or physical—against each other. (But the spirit of these shining moments in history were later perverted and turned on their head by the atrocities of the crusaders of the late Middle Ages.)

This passage from Psalm 30 was also beloved by the early Christians, those who survived persecution during those awful times, and the family and friends of those who were left behind.

> To you, O LORD, I cried,
>> and to the LORD I made supplication:
> "What profit is there in my death,
>> if I go down to the Pit?
> Will the dust praise you?
>> Will it tell of your faithfulness?
> Hear, O LORD, and be gracious to me!
>> O LORD, be my helper!"
>
> You have turned my mourning into dancing;
>> you have taken off my sackcloth
>> and clothed me with joy,
> so that my soul may praise you and not be silent.
>> O LORD my God, I will give thanks to you forever.
> (Psalm 30:8–12)

According to the legends of the church, martyrs enjoy an immediate and special place in heaven as a reward for their final deeds—Islam did not originate this idea. When Michelangelo painted his incredible *Last Judgment* on the altar wall of the

Sistine Chapel in Rome (1533–41), he pictured Christ as a Judge presiding over a vast scene, with the Virgin Mary to his right and famous martyrs to his left. Peter holds his papal keys; Catherine, the wheel that tortured her; Sebastian, a handful of arrows plucked from his body; Bartholomew, his own peeled skin in one hand and the knife used to do it in the other; and a few nameless saints hold the crosses on which they were crucified. Martyrs had a special place for eternity.

In the era of the martyrs it was easy to make a saint. A local bishop could name any martyr as someone to be remembered, imitated, and venerated. It was the decision of a local community, signified by a local bishop, to continue to "be in communion" (*communicarent*) with a man or a woman who had lived a holy life and died a noble death, confessing faith at the hands of others.

Martyrs were sainted so soon after their deaths during this period because the believers who were left living expected to see them again imminently. The early church was waiting for the prompt return of Jesus, and a community of saints was understood to be waiting in their graves to be reunited with the living. In these early days, from approximately 90 CE to the middle of the third century—just after the Gospel of John and some of the later epistles were written but before they were all collected into what became the accepted canon of the New Testament—the first Christians lived in heightened anticipation of the Second Coming, believing that the world would soon end. During these early days, the memory of the martyrs and their teachings were treasured but rarely preserved in any lasting way. Why bother to spend time and effort preserving memories of loved ones and friends when one expected to see them again so soon, in heaven? It would have seemed as foolish as buying lakefront property when you know that the world will soon be coming to an end. The apostle John seemed to know this when he wrote:

> "Very truly, I tell you, the hour is coming, and is now here, when the dead will hear the voice of the Son of God, and those who hear will live. For just as the Father has life in himself, so he has granted the Son also to have life in himself; and he has given him authority to execute judgment, because he is the Son of Man. Do not be astonished at this; for the hour is coming when all who are in their

graves will hear his voice and will come out—those who have done good, to the resurrection of life, and those who have done evil, to the resurrection of condemnation." (John 5:25–29)

This was part of the great hope that the apostle Paul had earlier given to the persecuted people of the church in Corinth:

Listen, I will tell you a mystery! We will not all die, but we will all be changed, in a moment, in the twinkling of an eye, at the last trumpet. For the trumpet will sound, and the dead will be raised imperishable, and we will be changed. For this perishable body must put on imperishability, and this mortal body must put on immortality. . . . [T]hen the saying that is written will be fulfilled:
"Death has been swallowed up in victory.
Where, O death, is your victory?
Where, O death, is your sting?"
(1 Corinthians 15:51–55)

The martyrs were not sullen people. They were full of joy, as were most of the communities that made up the early church. Death was something to celebrate, because it was the beginning of new life. Early Christians were not simply remembered at their funerals and never memorialized; they were cheered. Before the medieval devotion to saints really began, the first Christians knew joy in ways that were later lost. Even Christ's crucifixion was pictured by the early Christians as an almost serene event. In the earliest paintings and sculptures, Christ is pictured hanging there simply, his eyes wide open and facing forward, looking at you. The pain and torment of the cross was more a feature of medieval religion than a feature of the early church.

In Jesus' life there was great joy—in the wedding at Cana, in the shared meal at Mary and Martha's house, in the healings and the celebrations they created among the people who followed him. There was anguish for Jesus, too, as when he prayed all night on the Mount of Olives before he was arrested, and when he cried out from the cross. The spirituality of common people, however, did not incorporate an understanding of the pain Jesus experienced until after the time of the martyrs. Despite the obvious physical pain of martyrdom, and the emotional pain of witnessing the deaths of family and friends, and living on after they were gone, this was a joyful time for the church. They lived in anticipation.

Stephen was the first martyr. Jewish by birth, he was one of the most important early followers of the apostles after the death of Christ. He was a deacon of the early church and was stoned for preaching that Jews no longer needed the temple in Jerusalem or the law of Moses; these were temporary and were replaced by the person of Jesus Christ, he said (Acts 6). The stones that killed him, along with his bones, are still kept in Rome today. Stephen was also very beautiful. Many painted images of Stephen have been thought to border on the erotic, as they combine his violent death with the beauty of his physical appearance.

Polycarp was perhaps the most important martyr in the early church. He died in 155 and was the last personal disciple of one of the original twelve apostles (John). Polycarp was the bishop of Smyrna, in today's Turkey. He was the most venerable leader of the early Christians against heresy and was known for his early attempts to reconcile Eastern and Western Christian practice (such as the dating and celebration of Easter). Polycarp was martyred in Smyrna during a period when Christians were accused of atheism for their refusal to worship the emperor. Polycarp movingly refused to deny his faith before a crowd of his captors, and each step in the process of his trial and death was recorded by his own disciples.

Polycarp was burned at the stake, but witnesses said that the fire could not consume him. This caused the executioner to stab him with a dagger. So much blood flowed from his side that the fire was quenched with it, and, his disciples' record reads, "out came a dove" from his pierced body, a symbol to Christians that the soul lives on and flees straight to heaven.

The veneration of Polycarp—for his extraordinary witness and ministry to the faithful both before and after his martyrdom—began immediately after his death. In the *Epistle of the Church of Smyrna,* we read of how Polycarp's martyrdom came to be celebrated on the anniversary of his death (February 23):

> Thus we at last gathered up his bones, which are more precious to us than precious gems and finer than gold, and laid them to rest where it was proper to do so. There the Lord

will permit us to come together in gladness and joy to celebrate the birthday of his martyrdom.

Not all the martyrs lived during Roman times. One of the most famous martyrs in history is Thomas à Becket, who was born in London in 1118. While still in his thirties, Thomas was named chancellor of England by King Henry II, a post that made him both a personal adviser to the throne and an ambassador to the Vatican. Several years later, the king expanded Thomas's responsibilities by naming him archbishop of Canterbury. Pope Alexander III confirmed the appointment (for this was four hundred years before the Church of England split from Rome).

Thomas was a person of devotion, prayer, and real virtue. He strove to execute his duties to God and church with faithfulness, and, eventually, Thomas's independent spirit put him at odds with King Henry. After several disputes had pitted the two men against each other, and Thomas had fled England and then returned, the king announced, "Someone needs to rid me of my archbishop!" A group of knights, anxious for favors from the throne, rode to Canterbury and hunted Thomas down in the cathedral. He was a saint the moment his split head hit the cathedral floor; simple people gathered up his blood as relics as he lay dead.

Pilgrims began visiting Canterbury Cathedral as soon as word spread of the murder. The throngs were the medieval equivalent of the fans who gathered at the Dakota apartment building on New York City's Upper West Side after John Lennon's murder, or the thousands who visited Ground Zero in New York in the days and weeks following the September 11, 2001, terrorist attacks on the World Trade Center. In all three places today, at any given time, you will see cut flowers and other gifts brought as offerings, and written prayers left in cracks of flooring and sidewalk.

King Henry II himself traveled to Canterbury Cathedral less than four years after the murder that he had caused, doing penance for his sins. Four hundred years later, a much less penitent King Henry VIII ordered the shrine to Thomas razed so that pilgrimages might end and the monarchy of England might once again have spiritual (and temporal) authority over Rome within its shores. Thomas à Becket had made a fool of the monarchy of England four hundred years earlier, in Henry's perspective, by siding with the pope over the will of his earthly sovereign. Henry VIII did a bit of revisionist history in his proclamation of November 16, 1538, arguing that Thomas à Becket was indeed no martyr but was instead "a rebel and traitor to his prince." The proclamation went on to say:

> Therefore his grace [King Henry VIII] straightly charges and commands that from henceforth the said Thomas à Becket shall not be esteemed, named, reputed, or called a saint, but bishop Becket, and that his images and pictures, through the whole realm, shall be put down and removed out of all churches, chapels, and other places, and that from henceforth the days used to be festivals in his name shall not be observed, nor the service, office, antiphons, collects, and prayers in his name read, but razed and put out of all the books.

But as Henry learned, erasing the memory, memorials, and veneration of a saint is never so easy that it can be done by proclamation. Devotion to Thomas à Becket only grew. Martyrs have the power to effect great change through their deaths.

We also have Christian martyrs in our own time. Oscar Romero, the archbishop of San Salvador, was murdered on March 24, 1980, while celebrating Mass at the altar of a small hospital chapel. He was killed by a single gunshot to the chest by a soldier on the orders of a top El Salvadoran general.

Romero had united himself with the poor against the evils of El Salvador's military-ruled government, which had harassed and murdered hundreds of trade unionists, human-rights workers, priests, and others who spoke up against the atrocities. The United States, fearing the spread of communism in Latin America, supported the El Salvadoran government with arms and military advisers, even after Romero sent many pleas to then president Jimmy Carter, and even after Romero's murder. More killings occurred after Romero's death as well, including those of four Maryknoll and Ursuline nuns nine months later and six Jesuit priests, their housekeeper, and his daughter in 1989.

Like many martyrs before him, Romero knew that his death would take on special meaning. Two weeks before it happened, Romero told an interviewer: "I do not believe in death without resurrection. If they kill me, I will be resurrected in the Salvadoran people." He is already a saint in the eyes of the people of El Salvador, even though the process for his beatification, the second step to becoming a saint, appears to be moving very slowly in the Vatican. Jon Sobrino, a Jesuit theologian who would have been killed in 1989 along with the six Jesuit priests if he hadn't been away from home that evening, recently said: "Romero was like Jesus of Nazareth and the people who love Romero are the poor, those who have nothing. The rich are still afraid of him."[2]

In the pantheon of popular Protestant "saints," Martin Luther King Jr. is probably the most important of Americans from the last century. He, too, was martyred for his faith—in the cause of civil rights, in the potential of America to right its wrongs, and in Christ. People of all faiths would also be hard-pressed to deny Mahatma Gandhi, the great soul of India, sainthood in broader terms. As Gandhi tells in his autobiography, he was inspired to his nonviolent activism more by the Sermon on the Mount than by the Bhagavad Gita, the scripture of his native Hinduism, and his remarkable humanity was one with his saintliness, which led to his martyrdom.

Renaissance and modern saints who were martyred for their faith were no less joyful in life and death than their ancient forefathers and foremothers. Thomas More wished to his court judges at the Tower of London, who were about to convict him and sentence him to death, that one day they would all meet again in heaven. And despite Henry VIII's despicable behavior—allowing More, his old friend, to die for refusing to recognize his immoral second marriage and to accept him as "head" of the Church of England—More declared to his end that he was a faithful servant to the throne. Maria Goretti (d. 1902) was only twelve when she died from stab wounds inflicted by a young man who was attempting to molest her. She gladly forgave the man for his deed in the name of Jesus before she died. In the Orthodox tradition, there is the story of a Persian saint named James (d. 420s) who was tortured for professing his faith during a time of persecution of Christians. His limbs were stretched to breaking, and legend has it that he was cheerful and smiling until the end, when he was decapitated.

Since the earliest days, Christians have celebrated the death dates of saints, rather than their birthdays. This innovation, definitely not something inherited from earlier Jewish or pagan traditions, is distinctive to Christianity. The reason is very simple: a martyr's death day becomes, in effect, his or her new birthday, in heaven—a far more important occasion for celebration. Also, on the more practical side of things, the death day of a martyr was far easier to authenticate and remember than was his or her birthday.

It was during the rule of the Roman emperor Diocletian (284–305) that the first mention was made of the establishment of All Saints' Day, now November 1. During Diocletian's hideous rein, so many Christians were martyred that it became impossible to commemorate each on a specific day. All Saints Day was first established for the purpose of venerating them all.

Eventually, by the middle of the third century, the eschatological anticipations of the early Christians had lapsed, and a worldwide Christian movement was built. With it grew what has come to be called "the cult of saints"—that is, the preserving of their relics, the establishing of places where they should be venerated, and the spreading of their teachings. As one writer recently theorized, this interest in the saints grew "presumably from a desire for tangible links with a heaven that had come to seem more distant" than it did in the generations when some of the apostles were still alive.[3]

The Cult of Saints

THE APOSTLE PAUL URGED THE PEOPLE OF THE EMERGING church in Philippi to "join in imitating me, and observe those who live according to the example you have in us" (Philippians 3:17). The reverencing of model Christians made sense to the early church in the light of Paul's teaching. In following Jesus, Paul said, go ahead and imitate me. Death should not even separate us from one another, or any less from Christ. What is known as the cult of saints emerged in this context.

The word *cult,* when used to refer to those devoted to a saint, means "worship" or "reverence" (from the Latin word *cultus*). The cult of, or reverence of, saints spread rapidly throughout the Christian world in late antiquity. Relics of martyrs took on special meaning. Their bones—adored by the faithful but derided by critics as remnants of paganism—were compared by St. Augustine to the limbs of the Holy Spirit, holy and worthy of veneration. They were literally divided and parceled out throughout the Christian world in order to spread the goodness of the saint. It was not uncommon for a saint's finger to be in Paris, another finger in Cologne, his femur in London, and his head in Rome. St. Andrew, for example, who is the patron saint of Scotland, never stepped foot in any lands that far west; his missionary activity focused on Greece, Ukraine, and Russia in the years after the ascension of Christ. Andrew's bones, however, arrived in Scotland approximately four hundred years after his death in the first century. It also was common for two cities, competing for the best pilgrimage destination, to claim to have the same martyr's head.

Since the days of late antiquity, reverencing the saints has been a rubric for a distinctive ethos and spirituality of what it means to be Christian. Contemporary scholar Peter Brown explains:

> *Reverentia* [reverence] implied a willingness to focus belief on precise invisible persons, on Christ and his friends the saints . . . in such a way as to commit the believer to definite rhythms in his life (such as the observation of the holy days of the saints), to direct his attention to specific sites and objects (the shrines and relics of the saints), to react to illness and to danger by dependence on these invisible persons, and to remain constantly aware, in the play of human action around him, that good and bad fortune was directly related to good and bad relations with these invisible persons.[4]

Dead human beings signified an important link between heaven and earth. According to Aristotle, the stars we see above

26

the earth are fixed, divine, and what lies below them is mixed-up and corruptible, changing. The instance in which life turns to death is also an experience of heaven and earth meeting in the human body. A soul from beyond earth's confines joins with a body fashioned from clay at birth, and this lasts only for a time.

> The graves of the saints—whether these were the solemn rock tombs of the Jewish patriarchs in the Holy Land or, in Christian circles, tombs, fragments of bodies or, even, physical objects that had made contact with these bodies—were privileged places, where the contrasted poles of Heaven and Earth met.[5]

The distinction between body and soul was not perceived to be so great as to leave one unstained by the other. The divine soul continued to touch its human body after death and separation, in the way that a fine incense or rare spice can never be removed from the air or the dish that it seasons. The bodies of saints were held precious, because they were places where heaven met earth, places where miracles naturally happened, in both life and death.

Tombs were turned into holy altars in the cults of saints. Offerings were made and the Eucharistic sacrifice reenacted within view of the great fallen witnesses. They were venerated, and intercessory prayers were offered through them. Their tombs inspired everyday Christians to pray and to remember the holiness that is the goal of all people. The dead saint was believed to help one's communication with God, and the place of the grave was deemed sacred, a new holy of holies. The early church father Tertullian complained of some of these excesses barely 125 years after the death of the apostle John.

Jerome—scholar, hermit, and early apologist for the Christian faith—referred to the graves of early saints such as Peter and Paul as "altars of Christ." At their graves—and the other holy places associated with them—it is right and proper to offer sacrifices to God, Jerome argued. Such places, even and especially grave sites, became popular locations for ritual, ceremony, ornamentation, and miracles. The wonder-working powers of saints' bones—often preserved as relics in churches rather than buried—are well attested in popular medieval literature. The ninth-century historian Alcuin, wrote that the Venerable Bede's bones were curing people in Anglo-Saxon England. Such stories and beliefs were commonplace, even passed on by the most reliable of the era's scholars.

In a short review of "Byzantium: Faith and Power" (1261–1557), a 2004 Metropolitan Museum exhibit, the *New Yorker* magazine comically wrote: "[It] includes treasures like the 'Man of Sorrows' reliquary, filled with bits of saints tied in silk bags."[6] This sort of reliquary probably once drew thousands of pilgrims each year who were seeking healing, prayer, and other benefits associated with proximity to the physical presence of saints. Thousands of these reliquaries still exist in museums, cathedrals, and churches throughout the world. In fact, in 1999, Thérèse of Lisieux's reliquary visited 106 cities in the United States as part of a world tour to celebrate the centenary of her death.

Many churches were constructed around the bones of famous martyrs, and then, later, laying bones of martyrs to rest in churches also became common. Even today, there are several bone ossuaries, or depositories, in churches throughout Europe, where the bones of ordinary saints adorn the walls, light fixtures, and chalices and greet you at the entrance. Two of these—All Saints Church in Sedlec, Czech Republic, and Santa Maria della Concezione Church, in Italy—are popular tourist attractions drawing pilgrims from around the world. Such familiarity with bones is an important aspect of Christian spirituality, and has been throughout the ages, reminding us that death is another aspect of life that should be greeted without fear or dread.

Local cults of saints persist throughout the world today. In Brazil, for example, St. Expeditus is followed with great intensity. Popular images of the saint show him as a Roman soldier (who was supposedly martyred) holding a cross with the Latin word *Hodie* superimposed on it, which translates "today," and his with right foot crushing a black raven, which, according to another inscription, symbolizes "tomorrow." Expeditus is the chosen saint for prayers that need expeditious answers. Devotion to Expeditus, which has intensified in the last decade, has caused devotion to the saints in Brazil to resemble the pop-ularized, watered-down, Hollywood version of Kabbalah that has become faddish in the United States. In Brazil, the largest Catholic country in the world, church authorities as well as pop-culture icons embrace the saint of quick and convenient answers, even though Expeditus's existence is doubted by most scholars and he is not recognized by the Vatican. Stories abound in popular books and magazines and on television in Brazil explaining the values of devotion to St. Expeditus.

Honoring the dead, cherishing their remains or relics, and making pilgrimages to sites associated with their lives are also common in some Protestant circles. The Lutheran who travels to Wittenberg, Germany, cannot help but feel a deeper connection to the heart of the Lutheran faith. The Methodist or Wesleyan who visits Aldersgate, England, where John Wesley felt his heart "strangely warmed" for Christ, will often have a similar experience. In fact, the relics of key American church figures, such as Jonathan Edwards, George Whitefield, and Aimee Semple McPherson, have often been sought by congregations hoping to establish pilgrimage destinations. The primary difference between Catholic and Protestant expressions of devotion to the bodies of their saints is in the power appointed the saint after death. There is little evidence that Protestants believe that their saints might intercede with God on their behalf, or that healings might occur in these special places.

This reverencing of saints—not just the memory of them, or their witness and teachings, but their very bodies—makes more sense when we understand the radically different perspectives of the Protestant and the Catholic imaginations. We see the world with different eyes.

How I Came to Love
the Catholic Imagination

S A PROTESTANT CHILD, I WOULD HAVE READILY agreed with the answer to the first question of the Baltimore Catechism, a book that millions of Catholic children have learned in detail over the last one hundred years:

"Why did God make man?"

"Man is made to know, love, and serve God."

The issues of the present book do not center on whether or not this is the proper goal of our lives, but exactly how and to what extent we accomplish the task.

A rabbi friend of mine likes to explain that the most basic theological question is also the most important one: "Where do you live?" In other words, how you see the world around you, who you notice and who you do not, what qualities or characteristics you assign to your environment, and whether you view the universe as somehow sacred space or as cold and chaotic defines not only where you live but also who you are.

Some people see the world as full of saints. One of my favorite novelists, Nikos Kazantzakis, describes the changing of the seasons in the little town in Greece where he grew up in this way:

> Spring came with her fiancé Saint George mounted on a white steed, it left, summer came, and the Blessed Virgin reclined upon the fruited earth, that she too might rest after bearing such a son. Saint Dimitris arrived on a sorrel horse in the middle of the rains, dragging autumn behind him crowned with ivy and shriveled vine leaves. Winter pressed down upon us. . . . We were waiting for Christ to be born.[1]

For most Protestants, it would take a feat of imagination to approximate Kazantzakis's language. But for others, including many Catholics, it is natural to see the world that way. The Catholic imagination is not just a way of seeing the world; it is also an understanding that much of what we see and don't see will remain a mystery to us. The Catholic perspective would be that even those observations and stories that make no obvious immediate sense should remain a part of our lives. We should keep imagining. G. K. Chesterton explained:

> My first and last philosophy, that which I believe in with unbroken certainty, I learnt in the nursery. . . . The things I believed most then, the things I believe most now, are the things called fairy tales. They seem to me to be the entirely reasonable things. They are not fantasies: compared with them other things are fantastic. Compared with them religion and rationalism are both abnormal, though religion is abnormally right and rationalism abnormally wrong. Fairyland is nothing but the sunny country of common sense.[2]

I love the Catholic imagination. I am trying to see the world through Catholic eyes rather than with my Protestant ones. Andrew Greeley, the priest, novelist, and sociologist, explains the difference between the two this way:

> [T]he classic works of Catholic theologians and artists tend to emphasize the presence of God in the world, while the classic works of Protestant theologians tend to emphasize the absence of God from the world. The Catholic writers stress the nearness of God to His creation, the Protestant

32

writers the distance between God and His creation; the Protestants emphasize the risk of superstition and idolatry, the Catholics the dangers of a creation in which God is only marginally present. Or, to put the matter in different terms, Catholics tend to accentuate the immanence of God, Protestants the transcendence of God.[3]

The Catholic imagination has long distinguished itself as expansive, inclusive, and compelling. R. Scott Appleby, a historian at the University of Notre Dame, recently described it as "the capacious, sacramental religious imagination that operates by analogy rather than linear logic and perceives virtually everything human (including the body and sexual love) as occasion for a graced encounter with the divine mystery."[4]

Another scholar, expressing this in more theological terms, has explained: "Catholics see God's taking on flesh in the historical person of Jesus as God's own chosen way of coming to us in history—through physical and material reality. To Catholics, the entire world is sacrament, as the enfleshing of God."[5]

The Protestant imagination focuses on the gulf that separates us from God, while the Catholic view is of the sacramental nature of all that is around us. It is no wonder that while Protestant spirituality focuses on the Word of God (preaching it, hearing it, applying it) in order to repair the separation that divides us from God, Catholic spirituality focuses on finding, lifting, and releasing the Spirit of God that is sometimes hidden or latent in the world around us. This is the world as sacrament, the world incarnated.

Again, to quote Fr. Andrew Greeley, who is an expert in explaining theological distinctions in the clearest of language,

> Catholics live in an enchanted world, a world of statues and holy water, stained glass and votive candles, saints and religious medals, rosary beads, and holy pictures. But these Catholic paraphernalia are mere hints of a deeper and more pervasive religious sensibility which inclines Catholics to see the Holy lurking in creation. As Catholics, we find our houses and our world haunted by a sense that the objects, events, and persons of daily life are revelations of grace.[6]

33

Putting this more plainly, popular Catholic author Scott Hahn writes, "Catholics don't just hear the Gospel. In the liturgy, we hear, see, smell, and taste it."[7]

Where the Protestant approach to the Spirit is to analyze its meaning, the Catholic approach to the Spirit is to imagine its depths. Where the Protestant mind stops and pulls the strands apart, the Catholic mind makes further connections and intertwines the strands. My own approach to the Spirit and my own mind are clearly of the Protestant sort, but I wish it were not so. Many Protestants disdain "religion," by which they mean the trappings of religious celebration, or the sort of stuff one might find in a Catholic community on a saint's feast day. This eschewing of religion has harmed Protestants in some ways. We lack things and practices that would bind us together. Where the Protestant has mostly a religious outlook, the Catholic has a religion.

Carl Jung, the great psychiatrist, sensed this difference when he said, "I have treated many hundreds of patients, the larger number being Protestants. . . . It is safe to say that every one of them fell ill because he had lost that which the living religions of every age have given their followers and none of them has really been healed who did not regain his religious outlook." The Catholic imagination provides the support for living a spiritual life, not just a theological outlook.

The most important weekly Catholic magazine published in the United States, *America*, devoted much of its Lent/Easter 2003 issue to the perspectives of "contemporary Catholics on traditional devotions." Editor James Martin's comments sound like an invitation to Protestants as well:

> A surprising number of recent books and studies have suggested that young American Catholics are more likely than their immediate elders to gravitate toward traditional devotions. The reasons seem varied. Some surmise that younger Catholics, having grown up without being "forced" to participate in devotions, have no built-in reactions against them. Freer to embrace or ignore devotions, many choose to embrace them. Others see in this phenomenon a turn toward conservatism among younger Catholics. Still others posit that the characteristics of the

devotional life—tactile, colorful, often exotic—exert a particular influence on young Catholics seeking a greater sense of mystery in their lives.[8]

We live in a time when spiritually minded people of all backgrounds are seeking more and more to become spiritually practicing people as well. Catholics are able to translate their imagination into practice through the use of several traditional devotions, such as devotion to the saints.

The earliest Christian martyrs, after they were burned at the stake or torn apart by wild animals, had their bodies burned by Roman authorities, who wanted to limit the ability of their followers to venerate them. But Christians didn't need the bodies of the martyrs in order to venerate them. St. Gregory of Nyssa, one of the great teachers of the early Eastern church, explained: "Their ashes and whatever else remained were distributed throughout the provinces so that all might share in the blessing. I myself have a portion of these remains and had my own parents' bodies buried at the side of the ashes of these great Christian warriors so that when the resurrection comes they all may be awakened together." These sentiments, which were common in late antiquity and are still held by some Christians today (and, in slightly different fashion, by some Orthodox Jews who desire to be buried near the site of the second temple, where the Messiah is supposed to return), highlight the Catholic imagination. The saints are people we should want to be around, whom we can accompany, even lean on, and their physical presence, as well as their spiritual presence, can be keenly felt if we are receptive to them.

Gerard Manley Hopkins, the Anglican student turned Jesuit poet, thought of imagining as a contemplative exercise, a deliberate way of taking the world in and making sense of it with a spiritually inspired creativity; he called this "inscape." For Hopkins, it was possible to exercise the will in order to see the world and even create new interpretations of it by the guidance of the Holy Spirit. There is a danger, however, in bringing one's imagination to bear on one's spiritual life, and that is when "inscape" becomes too material. As many Protestants would point out, Catholic imagination often seems to lead toward a kind of Christian materialism, with all of its tactile objects of devotion, trinkets, and imaginative images, some of them quite fantastic.

For example, during Mother Teresa's beatification week in Rome, numerous trinkets made for the occasion were marketed on the streets. These included the Mother Teresa wall plaque ($29), a small triptych ($2.60), and a statue ($209.30).[9] Catholic cathedrals throughout Europe offer similar products for sale. In her biography of St. Thérèse of Lisieux, author Kathryn Harrison describes the kitsch to be found in Lisieux today, all of it dedicated to the saint: "racks of postcards and shelves of books, posters, prayer cards, votive candles, coffee mugs, snow globes, paper knives, tea towels."[10] The characters of the saints also offer myriad devotional options that are marketing tools for those who would make money off the desires of the faithful.

It often seems to Protestants that Catholic devotions, such as commemorating saints on their feast days and praying for the intercessions of saints, are for the sole purpose of asking favors of God. To Protestants, the spirituality of devotion to saints often seems aimed only at scoring well to overcome past failures and earning credit for future lapses. This seems to be the case, for instance, when Catholics receive Communion on the first Friday of the month for at least nine months in a row in order to ensure their eternal salvation, or when the devout wear the medal of St. Benedict so that God will grant them spiritual favors. Dom Gueranger, a French Benedictine monk, did the latter in his popular book *The Medal or Cross of St. Benedict: Its Origin, Meaning, and Privileges* (first English edition, 1880; reissued in 2002). Chapter 8 is entitled "On the Spiritual Favors Obtained by the Use of the Medal," and it chronicles healings of all kinds—physical, spiritual, and emotional—as well as conversions made possible when the medal was held in the hand. Similarly, I was once given a pamphlet of a novena (a special prayer to be prayed for nine days) to St. Jude. It promised that "prayer will be answered on or before the nineth day. Has never been known to fail!" Most Protestant objections to aspects of the Catholic imagination center on these practices. That is why Protestants so often use the word *excess* to describe Catholic pieties.

I admire the expansive spiritual imagination of Catholicism nonetheless. Where the eyes see, when the ears hear, what the nose smells, how the mouth tastes, and what the fingers touch are all different between our worldviews. I don't admire the rules and restrictions that have made these spiritual practices normative—as so often happens in religion—but I admire them at their most basic intentions. While many Protestants regard Catholic devotions as unnecessary, I am trying to incorporate them into my life, and many of these spiritual practices having to do with the saints are described throughout this book.

You'll recall the friend who asked me, "Why do you need all that extra stuff?" St. Francis de Sales says in *An Introduction to the Devout Life* that there is enormous value in spiritual practice that goes beyond what is simply enjoined us.

> Even as one who has just recovered from illness walks on a journey only as far as is absolutely necessary, so the repentant sinner treads in God's ways heavily and slowly until, having attained the grace of devotion, he resembles the healthy and light-hearted traveler who not only proceeds on his way, but runs, and leaps with joy.

The apostle Paul wrote this familiar passage in his first letter to the Corinthians:

> Love is patient; love is kind; love is not envious or boastful or arrogant or rude. It does not insist on its own way; it is not irritable or resentful; it does not rejoice in wrongdoing, but rejoices in the truth. It bears all things, believes all things, hopes all things, endures all things.
>
> Love never ends. But as for prophecies, they will come to an end; as for tongues, they will cease; as for knowledge, it will come to an end. For we know only in part, and we prophesy only in part; but when the complete comes, the partial will come to an end. (1 Corinthians 13:4–10)

In the meantime—until the complete comes—I want to learn to love God with my whole heart, mind, body, and spirit. I want to attain "the grace of devotion," as St. Francis de Sales so beautifully phrases it, and it seems to me that I will need to move beyond my Protestant imagination in order to do it.

Practices

Praying with and to the Saints

P RAYER IS THE MOST POPULAR AND ACCESSIBLE SPIRITUAL practice for relating to the saints. There is praying with the saints and praying *to* the saints. Each day, I do both, and neither practice means that I am forgetting that my relationship with God is accomplished through Jesus Christ.

When we pray to the saints it is never in the same spirit as how we pray to God; we never approach the saints as though they are prayer partners somehow similar to, or equivalent to, God. The saints make sense only as reflections in the mirror of the divine: they show God's glory. On All Saints' Day, Catholics pray in church: "God our Father, source of all holiness, the work of your hands is manifest in your saints, the beauty of your truth is reflected in their faith." In other words, without God, the lives of saints would seem ridiculous, but in the light of God's holiness, they begin to make sense.

Perhaps the most popular understanding of how we can relate to the saints is expressed in the phrase "St. _____, pray for us!" At times of urgent need and deep despair, we Christians often find the old forms of petitionary prayer on our lips. For Protestants, this often means quick prayers to God in Christ's name; for Catholics, it more often means praying to a special saint for help or guidance, believing that he or she has relevant experience to draw upon and can intercede for us in heaven.

The practice of praying to patron saints, those identified as helpful under particular circumstances, in certain places, and for special needs, is common. St. Christopher, for example, is the patron saint of truck drivers and cab drivers because of the legends of his helping travelers. Thomas More is the patron saint of politicians because he died a faithful one. The Archangel Gabriel is one of the patron saints of television because he brought the news of the Annunciation to the Blessed Virgin. Anthony of Padua is the patron saint for finding lost objects. And the campaign for the ideal patron saint of the Internet is ongoing. A recent CNN headline read, "Hopeless clickers urge Vatican to name protector," and *Newsday* reported that the two top candidates appear to be St. Isidore of Seville, the first encyclopedist of human knowledge (d. 636), and Rev. James Alberione, who has not yet been beatified or canonized but who championed the use of all new media for publishing religious materials and for evangelizing in the twentieth century.

The practice of appealing to patron saints can seem foolish or unnecessary at times, but how can one dispute that a saint, who is known for having overcome particular troubles and faced special difficulties, can offer us guidance in the same sort of situations? We may pray to the saints to illuminate our way with their example. I pray to St. Francis de Sales for patience and to St. Nicholas for the safety of my children. As with most prayers, our words have the power to change us more than to prompt heavenly action.

Examples of both types of prayer—*with* and *to* the saints—follow.

WITH THE WHOLE COMPANY
OF HEAVEN

We have the opportunity to pray with the angels as they intone these words continually in the presence of God (see Isaiah 6:1–4). Repeat this ancient prayer aloud to yourself or with others, knowing that you are joining with all the saints, both here and in heaven, and are recognizing and affirming with them that you are indeed a part of "the company of heaven."

Holy, holy, holy Lord,
God of power and might.
Heaven and earth are full of your glory.
Hosanna in the highest,
Hosanna in the highest.
(repeat three times)

TO BLESSED GABRIEL,
FOR HEAVENLY ASSISTANCE

Just as we pray to God through Christ, we may also pray for the spiritual aid of the saints who are already enjoying their heavenly reward. They are listening, and so are the angels who have always been God's messengers, connecting the divine and the human.

O blessed archangel Gabriel, we ask you to intercede for us
at the throne of divine mercy in our present necessities, that
as you announced to Mary the mystery of the Incarnation,
so through your prayers and patronage in heaven we may
obtain the benefits of the same, and sing the praise of God
forever in the land of the living. Amen.

TO ST. JUDE, PATRON
SAINT OF LOST CAUSES

Jude was a brother of James the apostle, and a friend of Jesus. Earliest tradition suggests that Jude had a gift and willingness for interceding directly with Jesus on behalf of others. Who is to say that Jude does not and cannot do the same today?

A chapel at St. Patrick's Cathedral in New York City has a near-life-size bronze statue of St. Jude. It is situated in the aisle of the nave on the north side of the famous church. St. Jude is standing, holding a staff and looking up to the heavens. This chapel with its statue of Jude is one of the most visited spots in the cathedral because Jude is one of the most popular saints the world over—and especially in the United States, since about the time of the Great Depression. Standing there on weekday mornings, I have seen people stop by to light a candle, pray, and often weep with emotion over their requests and needs. At a much simpler chapel in New Orleans, the popular singer Aaron Neville prays to St. Jude as part of his daily spiritual practice. Like millions of Americans, he credits the saint of hopeless causes with helping him overcome drug addiction and depression.

This simple prayer explains another reason why Jude is considered the patron saint of difficult circumstances and lost causes (see the third clause of the first sentence).

> Most holy apostle St. Jude, faithful servant and friend of Jesus, the name of the traitor who delivered the beloved Master into the hands of his enemies has caused you to be forgotten by many, but the church honors and invokes you

universally as the patron of hopeless cases, of things despaired of. Pray for me who am so miserable; make use, I implore you, of this particular privilege accorded to you, to bring visible and speedy help, where help is almost despaired of. Come to my assistance in this great need, that I may receive the consolations and succor of heaven in all my necessities, tribulations, and sufferings, particularly *(make your request here)*, and that I may bless God with you and all the elect forever.

I promise you, O blessed St. Jude, to be ever mindful of this great favor, and I will never cease to honor you as my special and powerful patron and to do all in my power to encourage devotion to you. Amen.

WITH ST. TERESA OF AVILA

This moving prose prayer was discovered in Teresa's breviary, or personal prayer book, after her death. The economy of words adds to its power, and the series of spiritual reminders are equally relevant for us today. (Teresa's original Spanish follows a simple English translation.)

Nothing disturbs thee,
Nothing frightens thee;
All things pass;
God never changes.
Patient endurance attains all things.
Nothing is wanting
in whom God possesses.
God alone suffices.

Nada te turbe,
Nada te espante;
Todo se pasa;
Dios no se muda.
La paciencia todo lo alcanza.
Quien a Dios tiene
Nada le falta.
Solo Dios basta.

An A to Z of the Famous
and the Not-So-Famous

The violent deaths of the martyrs make them heroes of our faith, but the stake and the executioner are not the only images for the making of saints. Almost every saint has his or her own symbol, whether he or she was a martyr, a lover of creation, a great teacher, a model of prayer, or a simple "flower" of God. Their images and their symbols tell us the stories of their lives. Francis of Assisi appears embarrassed over his delicately bleeding hands, feet, and side—as the bearer of the first stigmata, he was somehow afflicted with the five wounds of Christ. The great Jerome, a scholar and a solitary, sits with his equally great lion attendant; Jerome pulled a thorn from the beast's paw, giving birth to tales penned by storytellers from the Brothers Grimm to Walt Disney. The beautiful Lucia carries her lovely eyes, recently gouged out by her own hand, in a goblet so she can give them to the suitor whom she spurned and who then gave her up to martyrdom for being a Christian. And Lawrence, with an equal measure of nonchalance for his own fate, stands blithely beside the griddle that cooked him to a crisp. Without a doubt, there is something weird and alluring about the saints and their sometimes radical, extravagant lives for God.

The many cultural and historical categories of saints are as important as their symbols for telling the history of Christianity, both Eastern and Western. The earliest of saints, the apostles of Christ, who set out to tell the story of the life and ministry of Jesus around the world, are identified with intrepid courage. Most of them died at the hands of those whom they had come to save, and each of them—Peter, Andrew, James the son of Zebeedee, John, Philip, Bartholomew, Thomas, Matthew, James the son of Alphaeus, Thaddaeus, Simon, and Matthias (who replaced Judas)—is a saint. Next in the timeline we see the early martyrs, as described in chapter 2. They embodied the notion that this physical life is only temporary as they demonstrated with their lives and deaths that physical suffering is not to be feared.

After the era of the martyrs, whose blood is the foundation of the church, we enter the time of the desert fathers and mothers and other hermits—those unusual people who left behind the relative comfort of cities and families for a more severe experience of God. Learning from the example of some of the prophets in the Hebrew Scriptures, who lived alone for long lengths of time in the desert or the forest outside the city, Jesus also spent time alone in the wilderness and in the desert. John the Baptist, of course, did so as well. Hermits of the faith have always had one primary responsibility: to provide spiritual counsel, grounded in their prophetic distance from what is ordinary. Throughout the Middle Ages, for instance, anchorites and anchoresses lived as hermits in small rooms (or cells) attached to the outside of parish churches. One small window allowed the hermit to participate in worship, and another window faced out so that he or she could receive guests who sought wisdom. Blessed Julian of Norwich was an anchoress in England in the early fifteenth century. You can read more about her and other influential women of faith in chapter 11.

The first desert-hermit saint was Paul the Hermit (d. 342). Paul had another reason besides seeking a deeper experience of God for fleeing the city—to avoid generic faith and universalized religious practice, which had already begun to creep into the

Roman Empire in the decades following Constantine the Great's conversion to Christianity in 312 CE. According to tradition, a raven brought St. Paul, who lived in a cave, a loaf of bread from time to time. Antony of Egypt (d. 356), also known as St. Antony the Great, is recognized as the founder of monasticism. Like many saints before and after him, Antony was born into a wealthy and influential family but left that behind in order to pursue a deeper relationship with God. One legend has it that Antony made this decision one day after hearing Matthew 19:21 read during worship. When disciples began to gather around Antony, he was forced to abandon his solitary life and founded the first monastery, an interconnected set of hermit cells. We know a great deal about Antony because of the diligent work of Athanasius of Alexandria, his student and also a saint, who wrote the first hagiography on St. Antony in the middle of the fourth century. It was widely published and read even in those days long before paper and printing presses, and it influenced thousands of men and women to become monks and solitaries in the late Roman Empire.

The Meeting of St. Antony and St. Paul, *by Pinturicchio (d. 1513).*
The two old desert saints break bread together with many attendants—
other desert monks, angels, and St. Paul's raven—
outside of St. Paul's cave.

St. Benedict, *by Perugino (d. 1523), a painting in the Vatican Museums. The saint holds his quill and book, representing the influential Rule for monks that he authored.*

Benedict of Nursia (d. ca. 550) is recognized as the founder of monasticism in community. He, too, began his religious life as a hermit, but after spending several years alone in a cave in Italy (known today as *Sacro Speco*, "the holy grotto"), Benedict decided to found a "school of service" to God, a place where he would help other men lead holy lives through the monastic vocation. Named the patron saint of Europe for his role in schooling that region of the world in Christianity, Benedict learned from the hermits and monks who had come before him (Augustine, Basil the Great, John Cassian) and who had also written Rules, or guides, for the monastic life. Benedict's Rule became the norm for all of Western monasticism. It emphasizes the role of an abbot in strengthening a community of monks, the praying of the Divine Office in community, and the welcoming of guests as if they were Christ himself. He wrote his influential Rule while living in community, and within a few years he had founded at least twelve monasteries, which functioned like religious colleges for young and old alike. The feast of St. Benedict is celebrated each year on July 11. (More on the feasts of saints can be found on page 75ff.)

After the hermits in the time line of Christian saints, we see clearly the monks of sixth-and seventh-century Ireland. They were

An A to Z of the Famous and Not-So-Famous

known for their studiousness, and if it wasn't for their extraordinary dedication to copying and preserving the manuscripts of early Christianity, we wouldn't know much of what we now know about the first centuries of our faith. Hildegard of Bingen (d. 1179) should also be featured on any calendar of influential people of the Middle Ages. An accomplished musician, a Scripture scholar, and an author of books on subjects from hymnody to natural history to medicine, Hildegard was the abbess of a Benedictine community on the Rhine River. Her reputation as a rebuker of bishops and popes and her defiant burial of an excommunicated woman in the convent's cemetery have stood in the way of her being formally beatified or canonized by the Catholic church. Her cause for sainthood was active until about the year 1400; it should be reopened. The Anglican/Episcopal churches celebrate Hildegard's feast day on September 17.

A generation later we see the awakening of Italy, Europe, and all of Christendom by the selfless ministry of the *Poverello*, or "little poor man," from Assisi, St. Francis (d. 1226). He and his early spiritual brothers and sisters, the Franciscans and the Sisters of St. Clare, are the joyful fools of popular legend. Following the teachings of Jesus to the letter, they went about in want of nothing, and they were both revered and ridiculed for their simple lives. Despite their reputation as lighthearted and full of joy, the Franciscans also became known as great mediators of conflicts (during the Crusades and now in the West Bank of Israel/Palestine) and excellent scholars (they founded many of the first universities of Europe). There are many spiritual practices related to this most popular saint throughout this book.

Next we come to the remarkable saints produced by the Catholic Counter-Reformation in the sixteenth and early seventeenth centuries. St. John of the Cross (d. 1591) is, still today, an inspiration to many through his poetry and other writings on "the dark night of the soul," that darkness that is trusting faith and leads to deeper knowledge of God. And St. Ignatius of Loyola (d. 1556), author of the most influential book for Christian meditation ever written, the *Spiritual Exercises,* inspired Catholics to see the beauty and strength of their ancient tradition even after the reforms of Luther and others. He founded the Society of Jesus, the Jesuits, an order of religious men that desired to live an active (in the world) vocation, rather than a purely contemplative (in a cloister) one. Ignatius loved the stories of the early and medieval saints, although he occasionally disapproved of their asceticism and passiveness, and he taught their stories to thousands through his preaching. The Jesuits also focused their efforts on hearing confessions, urging personal conversion, and fighting heresy. Ignatius is the sort of saint the Catholic church in America needs today, a leader who would inspire new confidence in the truth of faith after the recent scandals.

It is remarkable that artists hardly ever figure among the saints, even those artists whose dedication to God and church seems to far surpass their ambition and passion for their art. Michelangelo would not fit in this category, although Lutherans celebrate him as a saint on April 6. But surely Palestrina and Thomas Tallis, composers of the Italian and Anglo-Saxon Renaissances, were—both were devout men and creators of exquisite, holy music, foundational in the history of worship. John Coltrane, the late jazz saxaphonist, would not be counted as a saint on any of the major calendars, but his inspired creativity, rehabilitation from alcohol and heroin addiction, and mystical conversion late in life inspired a San Francisco church to name itself for him and to erect enormous icons with his image. The St. John Coltrane African Orthodox Church is a charter member of the African Orthodox church and has been the subject of stories in national and international news media.

We might ask: What are the qualities or characteristics most common in saints throughout history? Who has the greatest likelihood of achieving special recognition for sanctity? The realm of sainthood can seem like a closed society available only to virgins, martyrs, solitaries, and stylites. We resist the notion that what was virtuous for one person in one situation should necessarily be just as virtuous in all situations, times, and places. We don't like easy checklists, such as the one that seems to be used to determine whether to beatify or canonize someone. A cursory look at the roster of Catholic saints might lead us to conclude that somewhere there is a list such as this one:

virginity	good
martyrdom	good

solitariness	good
family life	bad
stylitic life	good
home ownership	bad
hearing voices	good
parenthood	bad
penance	good
happiness	question motives
asceticism	good
miracles	good
persistent doubt	bad
visions	good (usually)
compassion	good
sexuality	definitely bad
heroic virtue	good
laughter	bad (usually)
seriousness	good

Of course, there are no such criteria. We will look at saints—even some loved by the church—who defy these categories and common assumptions. There are thousands of saints, and I hope this book will turn you toward the many remarkable resources available for learning more about them.

We have no written record of what Polycarp looked like. We know very little about Augustine's face and George's physique, and we know almost nothing about Mary Magdalene and Mary of Egypt, except that they were beautiful and desired by men. Thomas of Celano, Francis of Assisi's first biographer and his contemporary, wrote these loving lines about the little poor man from Assisi:

> He was eloquent and had a cheerful appearance and a kind face, free of laziness or arrogance. He was of medium height, closer to short, and his head was of medium size and round. His face appeared drawn, forehead small and smooth, medium-sized eyes, black and clear. His hair was dark; eyebrows straight, his nose even and thin. His tongue was peaceable, fiery and sharp; his voice was powerful, but pleasing, clear, and musical. His teeth were white, well set and even, his lips were small and thin; his beard black and sparse. His neck was thin, shoulders straight, arms short,

and hands slight. He had thin legs, small feet, fine skin, and very little flesh. His clothing was rough, sleep short, and his hand generous.

We are not so fortunate to have this level of description of many other popular saints.

Icon painters must paint faces of saints all the time. Since most icons are copies of paradigmatic icons painted long ago, we often find a fair degree of similarity from one icon to the next. One popular painter's manual, passed down from teacher to student for the last three centuries on Mount Athos, the monastic republic on the Greek peninsula of Athos, offers this sage advice about how to represent each of the popular stylites:

> Saint Simeon Thaumastooreites, an old man with a rounded beard.
> Saint Simeon Stylites, an old man with a short beard divided into two points.
> Saint Daniel Stylites, an old man with a pointed beard.
> Saint Alypius Cionites, an old man with a long beard.
> Saint Luke the young stylite, grey-haired, with a beard divided into two points.[1]

It would seem that facial hair was the primary way to distinguish a saint of this type.

In truth, an icon painter will tell you that it is the eyes of the figure—which are intended to be a presence of the person represented—that are the most important feature, and the last thing painted. If you connect with the eyes in an icon, if they seem perhaps to "speak" to you, that icon and that saint may be meaningful for your vocation and situation in life. Icons can convey a sense that the saints they represent are immediately present with you.

What we have in abundance, instead of accurate images, are stories of the saints. Hopefully, you will connect with at least one of the following stories in the way that you might connect with an icon. These tales, some historically reliable and others uncertain, are what binds Christians to one another. Many of them began as oral tradition and were later written down for the ease of memory. The short profiles that follow, of saints not already mentioned, represent a wide cross-section of Christians throughout the ages and the world—men and women, ancient and modern, East and West, North and South, strange and typical.

Andrew Kim Tae-gon. Korean Catholics are rightly proud of the origins of the Catholic faith in Korea; it was built on the blood of martyrs, much as was the church of the West almost two millenia earlier. Andrew (d. 1846) was the first native Korean priest, having been ordained by French missionaries in Shanghai, China. Christianity was illegal in Korea at this time, and nearly one hundred people had been martyred there since the beginning of the nineteenth century. "The usual method of martyrdom was to be tied to a cross, taken on an oxcart to the place of execution, stripped naked, and then beheaded. Their heads and bodies would be publicly exposed for three days to terrify other Christians."[2] Within days of his ordination, Andrew returned to Korea as a leader of the underground movement. Soon, he was captured and thrown into prison, where he wrote a pastoral letter that sustained the fledgling church, much as the apostle Paul's letters, written while he was in prison, sustained the early church. Andrew was martyred, and 138 years later Pope John Paul II canonized him from the Seoul Cathedral.

Brendan. Known as the sailor-monk, or the seafaring saint, Brendan (d. ca. 575) spent most of his adult life in a boat with the men who followed him, sailing from island to island in the Irish Sea. He founded monastic communities wherever he went, which may have included Scotland, Wales, and parts of Britain as well. Brendan's navigations became legendary; like the stories of Beowulf, they were repeated for centuries. These charming tales liken the places of Brendan's sea travels, which were often islands either lovely or uninhabitable, with inhabitants either friendly or hostile, to places of the Apocalypse (heaven, purgatory, hell). Other tales relate non-spiritual myths, such as the one in which Brendan and his fellow seafaring monks land on an island and, upon kindling a fire, realize that the island is not in fact solid land but rather an enormous sea monster.

Catherine of Siena. Known as the great debater, Catherine (d. 1380) is one of the most charming figures in history. She is a fine example of an independent theologian in the medieval church. She converted pagan philosophers and argued with popes (Pope Urban VI's men once even tried to arrange for her murder, unsuccessfully). Always criticized by men for having strong opinions and presuming to teach, Catherine once retorted to a bishop that he was ordaining "boys and not men" to be priests. She was declared a doctor of the church in 1970, an honor long overdue, and her life as a saint is celebrated by Episcopalian and Lutheran (ELCA) churches in the United States, as well as by the Catholic church.

Dismas the Good Thief. The last person Jesus spoke to before he died on the cross (Luke 23:39–43), Dismas was considered a saint by the early church on account of his clear faith in Jesus as the Son of God. (The Scriptures do not give us Dismas's name, however; tradition does that.) Jesus was a friend to sinners, and perhaps Dismas had heard Christ's teachings before that day on Golgotha, when Dismas said to him, "Jesus, remember me when you come into your kingdom." Jesus replied, "[T]oday you will be with me in Paradise." The early church regarded the day of their death and new life as March 25.

Elizabeth Ann Seton. The first American-born person to be canonized, in 1975, Elizabeth was born two centuries earlier in New York City as the American colonies were heading to war with England. She was the child of devout Anglican parents, and she became known as "the Protestant sister of charity" as a young married woman, when she used her substantive resources to aid widows and children. When her husband, William, went suddenly bankrupt and soon after died of tuberculosis, Elizabeth converted to Catholicism. It was 1805, and there were relatively few Catholics in the United States; she was almost thirty years old. A few years later, she founded the Daughters of Charity, a religious community for women, and became known as Mother Seton for her caring and able approach to both administrative duties and personal relationships. The order founded schools for needy children, charging tuition only to those who could afford it.

Frances Xavier Cabrini. Another American saint, Mother Frances became the patron saint of immigrants, as she devoted her life to caring for those who came to this country, largely from European countries, in the late nineteenth and early twentieth centuries. An immigrant herself, from Italy, she came to the United States in 1889. She was canonized immediately following the Second World War.

George Herbert. An Anglican priest of the early seventeenth century, Herbert's life is celebrated by both the Anglican/Episcopal church and the Lutheran (ELCA) church in America. He influenced many of the great religious writers in England who came after him, both Protestant and Catholic, including the poets Henry Vaughan, John Milton, and Gerard Manley Hopkins and the hymn writer Charles Wesley. His images, such as those in this famous poem of metaphors about prayer, have informed the English-language, devotional tradition more than any other poet:

> Prayer the Church's banquet, Angels age,
>> God's breath in man returning to his birth,
>> The soul in paraphrase, heart in pilgrimage,
> The Christian plummet sounding heav'n and earth;
> Engine against th' Almighty, sinners tower,
>> Reversed thunder, Christ-side-piercing spear,
>> The six-days world transposing in an hour,
> A kind of tune, which all things hear and fear;
> Softness, and peace, and joy, and love, and bliss,
>> Exalted Manna, gladness of the best,
>> Heaven in ordinary, man well dressed,
> The milky way, the bird of Paradise,
>> Church-bells beyond the stars heard, the soul's blood,
>> The land of spices; something understood.

Helena. Her life is a fascinating combination of fact and fiction; whether true or not, her story is one of the most important tales of the Roman era of the church. Helena's son, Constantine, became the first Christian emperor of the Roman Empire in 312 after earning a victory in battle that he felt God had given him. Helena converted to Christ with her son, as did much of the

The Vision of St. Helena, *by Paolo Veronese (d. 1588).*
Two child angels show the saint the whereabouts
of the true cross in a dream.

empire. Several years later, as part of her new devotion to God, Helena made a pilgrimage to the Holy Land. Having been told in a dream the whereabouts of the true cross of Christ, she led an excavation to unearth it. With the cooperation of Macarius, the bishop of Jerusalem and later a saint himself, and with the aid of the power represented by her son, Helena first destroyed the heathen temple to Venus that stood on Calvary at that time. Eventually, after much digging, the cross of Christ, as well as those of the two thieves, was found, and according to legend, the nails and the inscription board that had been hung above our Lord were discovered as well.

Ivo of Kermartin. There are very few civil lawyers on the calendar of saints. Ivo (d. 1303) was a lawyer in France at a time when corruption was taken for granted and impartiality was almost nonexistent. A model for how the law should function in any age, Ivo, who was trained as both a canon (religious) and a civil judge, advocated settlements out of court whenever possible. He practiced a strict, monastic-style spirituality in order to ensure that his motivations were as righteous as possible. He was known as a defender of the poor, or those who could not afford adequate legal representation, and as a pardoner who always sought to give people a second chance whenever possible. Toward the end of his life, Ivo also became a priest.

Jerome. A symbol of both repentance and scholarship, Jerome was a serious student of the classics when he was converted to a desire to know the Scriptures instead. He was the first to translate the Bible into Latin (known as the Vulgate), and he is known to history as one of the four Latin doctors of the church (with Ambrose, Augustine, and Gregory the Great). He was cantankerous and ill-mannered toward those in authority, and he did not last long in Rome. When his friend Pope Damasus died, Jerome settled in Bethlehem and eventually founded a monastery there, near the birthplace of Jesus. Jerome died in about 420.

St. Jerome in the Desert, *by Lord Frederic Leighton (d. 1896).*
The saint performs penance in the wilderness before a cross of his
own making while his faithful lion faces the sunset.

Katharine Drexel. One of 137 Americans beatified or canonized as of the end of 2003, this Philadelphian died in 1955. She was known as Mother Katharine throughout her religious life, which formally began at age thirty when she joined the Sisters of Mercy as a nun. The child of wealthy parents (her father was a banker who left her a fortune in the millions), Katharine gave her assets and herself completely to the poor. She was specifically drawn to the plight of Native Americans throughout the U.S. West and African Americans in U.S. cities, who suffered from poverty and a lack of educational resources. In 1891 she founded a new religious congregation (similar to an order) called Sisters of the Blessed Sacrament. The sisters built schools—more than one hundred of them. Mother Katharine and her sisters were an important part of the early civil rights movement in America and were often threatened by the Ku Klux Klan. Richard P. McBrien, a Catholic scholar recounts the following anecdote: "Her sisters walked the streets of New Orleans and Harlem during the 1950s and were jeered at and called 'Nigger sisters.' When they described the name-calling to Mother Katharine, she simply asked, 'Did you pray for them?'"[3]

 Louis-Marie Grignion de Montfort. Known for his extraordinary devotion to the Virgin Mary, Montfort authored the most important book in the history of Mariology, *True Devotion to Mary.* Published for the first time in 1842, the book went out of print and remained unpublished for nearly 150 years (a portion of the book appears on pages 79-80). He was born in Brittany, France, in a small town named Montfort, from which he took his surname. He was ordained a priest in 1700, and his primary vocation was as a "missionary apostolic," or traveling preacher. Louis de Montfort founded two religious orders, both of which are active in the United States today: the Montfort Fathers and the Brothers and the Daughters of Wisdom, who run the Wisdom House Retreat and Conference Center in Litchfield, Connecticut.

Mary Magdalene. Considered to be one of the true apostles of Christ, Mary Magdalene is one of the most fascinating saints in history. Interest in her life and her role in Jesus' life has been sparked in recent years by Dan Brown's best-selling novel *The Da*

Vinci Code. Some legends identify her with the prostitute in Luke 7 and with the woman who perfumed the feet of Jesus in John 12; other legends, even less reliable, suggest that she had an intimate relationship with Jesus. In any case, Mary Magdalene was the most important witness of the Resurrection, according to the Gospel accounts. She was a disciple of Jesus and a friend and adviser of the first apostles.

Paintings of Mary Magdalene always show her physical beauty. Here she holds a lamp, an image of her waiting and looking for the resurrected Lord. St. Clare of Assisi is beside her in this painting by Luca Signorelli (d. 1523).

Nicholas of Flüe. The patron saint of Switzerland was quite a different character from the patron saint of Norway (see "Olaf, King of Norway," next entry). He was a hermit, a layperson, and the father of ten children. These are remarkable facts taken together, and Nicholas was a remarkable and enigmatic figure. He was a local government leader, employed as a magistrate while still a young man. But while his children were still at home, his wife gave him permission to live much of the time in a small hermitage, practicing various forms of asceticism (he reportedly ate only the Eucharist for many years) and meditating on the Passion, as did many other members of the

Friends of God, a lay movement once popular throughout Switzerland. During his stays in the hermitage, Nicholas became a popular spiritual director, even advising government officials to the point of helping the country avoid a civil war.

Olaf, King of Norway. Norwegian Lutherans celebrate Olaf, the patron saint of Norway as an example of how patriotism can affect our feelings about sanctity. A brutal man, Olaf used the sword to convert his people to Christianity and was himself ultimately killed in battle in 1030. (Other countries have militant patron saints as well. Spain's patron is Santiago Matomoro, St. James the Moorslayer, a reference to the battle between Christians and Muslims in Spain that unfortunately continues today.) My own prejudices lead me to see **Flannery O'Connor,** the twentieth-century American writer, as deserving saintly recognition. A devout Catholic, her fiction startles with its use of sometimes violent and always arresting images and characters who find God's grace in the unlikeliest of places.

Pierre Toussaint. Born into slavery on the French colony of Santo Domingo (modern-day Haiti), Pierre was purchased by Marie Elizabeth Berard and taken to New York City in 1787. Pierre worked as a hairdresser there and was soon in demand among New York's elite. Pierre was able to make and save some money. He purchased his sister's freedom from their master, but did not purchase his own. Berard had been recently widowed, and Pierre appears to have willingly chosen to remain a slave in order to care for her and allow her to avoid embarrassment. Finally granted his own freedom when Berard passed away, Pierre married Juliette Noel, whose freedom he had also purchased. He spent the rest of his years making money in order to give it away. Pierre was dedicated to aiding immigrants new to America; he housed orphans, schooled black children he discovered on the streets, and cared for plague victims, as Mother Teresa later did in Calcutta. He died at about the age of ninety in 1853. His case for sainthood was opened in 1968, and in 1990 his body was exhumed and reburied under the main altar of St. Patrick's Cathedral in New York City.

Queen of Heaven. The Virgin Mary has long been celebrated as the "Queen of Heaven"; in fact, the Christians of the late Roman Empire most likely adopted the term from popular religion, as the goddess Isis (and others) also held the honorable title. The title "Queen of Heaven" recognizes Mary's role as "blessed among women" (as uttered in the Hail Mary) and as (queen) mother to the child who assumed "the throne of his ancestor David" (Luke 1:32). It was not until the mid-twentieth century that the Catholic church made a special feast day for the Queen of Heaven, reminding Catholics of her leadership role over angels, patriarchs, prophets, apostles, martyrs, confessors, virgins, and all saints, as prayed for centuries in the Litany of the Blessed Virgin, approved by Pope Xystus (or Sixtus) V in 1587. One of the most popular Roman Catholic hymns is the *Salve Regina,* or "Hail Holy Queen." Many churches have adopted the name, such as Our Lady Queen of Heaven Catholic Church and Mary Queen of Heaven Catholic Church.

Rita of Cascia. It is no wonder that, in the lives of saints, one of the common meanings of *saint* focuses on sweet forbearance in the midst of terrible trouble. We look at a child who smiles despite suffering and say, "She is such a saint!" St. Rita is one saint who gives rise to such pronouncements; her life was so pathetically sad. She was married for eighteen years to an unfaithful and abusive husband. One night, he was murdered, and soon afterward, Rita's only two children, both sons, also died. Childless and widowed, she became a nun and devoted herself to prayer. It is said that Rita prayed and meditated so fervently on the Passion that she received wounds on her forehead like those of Christ from the crown of thorns. Rita eventually died of tuberculosis (in 1447), but immediately after her death she became renowned for intercessory miracles. She joins St. Jude as the other popular saint of desperate causes.

Seven. There are four **Sevens** among the saints. First are the **Seven Apostles of Bulgaria,** seven men who brought Christianity to the Slavs in the Middle Ages. Then there are the **Seven Brothers.** According to legend, these sons of Felicity, also a saint, were each martyred during one of the early Roman persecutions of

61

Christians. As the story goes, Felicity witnessed each execution before her own life was taken. The **Seven Servite Founders** were devout men from wealthy homes in thirteenth-century Florence who formed a new religious order of friars after the example of St. Francis of Assisi, but they were devoted to honoring the Virgin Mary. They emphasized Mary's "seven sorrows" as well as her "seven joys." Finally, there are the **Seven Sleepers of Ephesus**. These men of Ephesus reputedly slept for two hundred years in a cave on Mount Celion,—from the time of Roman persecution under Emperor Decius to the day when the region was ruled by Christianity—woke up, and promptly died. Their legend, told by St. Gregory the Great, concludes with the seven sleepers happily buried in the same cave.

Teresa/Thérèse. We will discuss three Teresas elsewhere in this book: Teresa of Avila, Thérèse of Lisieux, and Teresa of Calcutta. They are undoubtedly three of the most important saints in the last 500 years.

Thomas. The two Thomases mentioned here are both profound writers in the history of Christian theology or spirituality. **Thomas Aquinas** (d. 1274) was a Dominican friar and theologian—the most influential theologian, in fact, in the history of the Catholic church. Highborn in a family of knights and landowners, Thomas was drawn to join the mendicant order of the Dominicans as a young man. His family resisted his wishes and actually imprisoned him for a year in an effort to change his mind. Thomas Aquinas was known for his remarkable ability to concentrate, which aided both his scholarship and his meditation. It was said that he would often dictate to four scribes at once so that the flow of his ideas would not have to be slowed by the time it took a person to record them. His greatest work, the multivolume *Summa Theologica,* sought to blend the ideas of the Greek philosophers Aristotle and Plato with the teachings of Holy Scripture and the early church fathers. Based on these ideas, Thomas and his mentor, Albertus Magnus (Albert the Great), created Scholasticism, the most dominant method in the history of theology. **Thomas à Kempis** (d. 1471) led a very quiet life by comparison. A Flemish hermit, he wrote a simple book,

The Imitation of Christ, that became the most widely read spiritual book of all times, next to the Bible itself. Although by all accounts he experienced very little of the world for himself, Thomas's understanding of the human heart is second to none. His classic book was first published anonymously in 1418. His candidacy for beatification has unfortunately lain dormant since the seventeenth century.

Ursula. Her legend is one of the most tragic of the Middle Ages and points to the medieval mind's fascination with sexuality. This bold young Anglo-Saxon woman (lived ca. fourth century) was engaged to marry a heathen prince against her will. She wanted nothing but a life of perpetual virginity and fidelity to Christ. She and several of her like-minded maiden friends, with thousands of other attendant virgins, sailed down the Rhine River through Cologne as pilgrims to Rome. Upon their return to Cologne, the women were violated and martyred by a band of Huns who had waited for them. Later mystics claimed to see visions that corroborated this story, and in 1155 thousands of bones were discovered and claimed to be those of the young women. A church was built in their honor in Cologne, and the cult of Ursula and her companions remains strong in the Low Countries and France.

Ursula and the other maidens arrive by ship in Cologne in this painting by Hans Memling (d. 1494).

Valentine. This saint is just one example of how near-anonymous saints have taken on greater meaning in popular culture. We know almost nothing about St. Valentine, except that he was a martyr of the early church, most likely during the infamous persecutions led by the Roman Emperor Decius, who ruled for only two years, from 249 to 251. There are not even reliable legends about Valentine, although he has come to inspire love in millions (at least on one day of the year). Similarly, we know very little about St. Nicholas of Myra, named for a provincial capital in what is today the country of Turkey. The inspiration for the modern Santa Claus, Nicholas is also the patron saint of Russia and Greece. Nearly all churches—Catholic, Orthodox, and Protestant—that recognize saints, celebrate the feast day of St. Nicholas on December 6. Valentine is not so fortunate; his name no longer appears on any calendars of saints.

Wang Cheng. The Boxer Rebellion in China (1898–1900) saw the murder of many Christians. It was an anti-Western movement that also encompassed a revolt against the missionary efforts of Christians to convert Chinese. Four girls in their teens were among the martyrs. Raised in a Catholic orphanage in Wangla village, part of Hebei province, where a large wave of killings occurred, these girls were taken hostage rather than immediately killed, probably because of their youthful beauty. One of the Boxer leaders proposed marriage to Wang Cheng, who at eighteen was the eldest of the four, and she rejected him. The other girls were sixteen, fifteen, and eleven years old. After about a week of moving the young hostages around to various locations, the Boxer rebels finally returned them to their village of Wangla and demanded that they renounce Christ. They refused, saying, "We are daughters of God. We will not betray him," so they were murdered. John Paul II canonized all 120 martyrs of China (eighty-seven Chinese and thirty-three missionaries, mostly Franciscan), including Wang Cheng, on October 1, 2000.

Xystus. Many popes are saints, but not all of them are. When elected, each pope takes a new name, and it has been common for popes to take the name of a previous pope, recognizing him as a spiritual forefather. **Xystus I** (d. ca. 127), whose name is anglicized to Sixtus I, was one of the first popes and led the early church during the persecutions of the Roman emperor Trajan. **Xystus II** (d. 258) was pope for only a year and was also martyred, beheaded and buried in the Roman catacombs. He is often pictured in religious art with St. Lawrence, his contemporary. Before he was martyred, Xystus II met with Lawrence, an archdeacon, and turned over the wealth of the papacy to him so that Lawrence might distribute the treasures to the poor and the needy. Four days later, Lawrence was summoned and told to bring with him the treasures of the church. Dozens of previously hidden congregants joined Lawrence that day, symbolizing the true meaning of the church, but they were turned away in anger, and Lawrence was killed. **Xystus III** (d. 440) was a friend and correspondent of Augustine of Hippo, with whom he battled against many heretic groups of the day. He had the benefit of dying a natural death eight years into his pontificate. There were two more Sixtus popes, both from the Renaissance era, who have little to recommend them: Sixtus **IV** (d. 1484) and Sixtus **V** (d. 1590).

Ywi. An Irish monk of the mid-seventh century, Ywi lived in self-imposed exile for Christ, according to the model established by St. Cuthbert, the great monk of Lindisfarne, who was his teacher. Ywi, whose name is also rendered Iwi, wandered the seas with no set course or destination, expecting to spread the Good News wherever he might land and with whomever he might meet.

Zeno. Not to be confused with the ancient philosopher known by the same name, Zeno (d. 371) was born in Africa and was an excellent fisherman. He fished to feed himself while he was a hermit living along the river near Verona, Italy. Zeno fought against heresies in the church and encouraged young people to commit themselves to serving God through various ministries. He was an excellent pastor, the first bishop of Verona, and a hard worker. We also know that Zeno loved a good belly laugh; he was perhaps the first of the saints to show real outward joy, through laughter, as a part of his spiritual practice.

Three Late-Twentieth-Century
Saints in the Making

WE WILL ALWAYS HAVE SAINTS IN THE MAKING, THOSE WHOSE cases for sainthood are being prepared by local dioceses and brought to the attention of Vatican authorities. The pope is always being pressed to consider the worthiness of candidates, and the Orthodox churches, although they have a different process for recognizing saints, are always considering candidates for saintly recognition as well. Some popular twentieth-century causes have been under way for years, even for several decades and many (Dorothy Day, Oscar Romero, and even non-Catholics such as Albert Schweitzer and Mahatma Gandhi) are discussed elsewhere in this book. The following three lesser-known figures are each remarkable for their commitment to justice and interreligious reconciliation.

MOTHER MARIA SKOBTSOVA

Few people would argue with the cause for sainthood of Mother Maria Skobtsova. She is a Russian Orthodox saint in the making. Born Elizaveta Pilenko in Latvia in 1891, she became Mother Maria after a lifetime of remarkable experiences. Almost executed during the 1917 Russian Revolution, Elizaveta was a leader in local government, a twice-married mother of three children, and a political refugee who fled the turbulent Russian Empire for France in 1919. After her second daughter died of illness, Elizaveta, one of those amazing people who could turn unspeakable tragedy into an opportunity for deepening holiness, began to feel a calling to a more "broad and all-embracing motherhood."[4] As an exile in Paris, Elizaveta became fully committed to the plight of the poor, the dispossessed, the mentally ill, and anyone in need, most importantly, Jews who were forced to hide during the Nazi occupation. Mother Maria served those in need until she too was gassed in the Nazi concentration camp in Ravensbrück, Germany.

Mother Maria wrote these inspiring words:

> It would be an unseemly protestantizing on the part of
> Orthodox people if they forgot . . . man is not alone and
> his path to salvation is not solitary; he is a member of the
> Body of Christ, he shares the fate of his brothers in Christ,
> he is justified by the righteous and bears responsibility for
> the sins of the sinners. The Orthodox Church is not a
> solitary standing before God, but *sobornost'*, which binds
> everyone with the bonds of Christ's love and the love for
> one another.
>
> Anyone who loves the world, anyone who lays down
> his soul for others, anyone who is ready, at the price of
> being separated from Christ, to gain salvation for his
> brothers—is a disciple and follower of Christ. And
> inversely, anyone who abides in the temptation of self-
> salvation alone, anyone who does not take upon himself
> the responsibility for the pain and sin of the world, anyone
> who follows the path of "egoism," be it even "holy" egoism,
> simply does not hear what Christ says, and does not see
> what His sacrifice on Golgotha was offered for.[5]

JOSEPH CARDINAL BERNARDIN

The archbishop of Chicago from 1982 until his death from
pancreatic cancer in 1996, Bernardin (b. 1928) was named a
cardinal by Pope John Paul II. A man of great humility and
concern for others, "Brother Joseph" was an outspoken opponent
of nuclear proliferation, a leader in Jewish-Catholic dialogue and
relations, and one of the most remarkable pastoral consensus
builders that the Catholic church in America has ever produced.

Bernardin created the Catholic Common Ground Project in
the last decade of his life in an attempt to reconcile liberal and
conservative voices in the church. In an October 1996 public
address to introduce the intiative, Bernardin articulated some of
the "conditions for a renewed and successful dialogue among
U.S. Catholics." These included: "that our discussions assume
the need for boundaries, distinctions, and defining limits, even
where these may be open to reexamination; that we recognize

no single group as possessing a monopoly on solutions to the Church's problems or the right to spurn the mass of Catholics and their leaders as unfaithful; that we test proposals for pastoral realism; that we presume those with whom we differ to be in good faith and put the best possible construction on their positions; that, above all, we keep the liturgy, our common worship, from becoming a battleground for confrontation and polarization."[6] He is remembered as one of the great pastoral leaders of the last century.

CARDINAL FRANZ KÖNIG

Made a cardinal by Pope John XXIII, König passed away at age ninety-eight in 2004. He was the last living cardinal who participated in the Second Vatican Council. König was one of the most outspoken advocates among Catholic leaders for inter-religious dialogue as well as for some issues that are of utmost importance to much of the laity in America today. "Well into his 90s, he continued calling for decentralization of power within the Catholic Church, for greater collegiality among the world's bishops and for a broader involvement of priests and laity in the nomination of bishops," wrote the Catholic News Service in his obituary.

While archbishop of Austria, a post he held for thirty years, König reached out to Jews with friendship, to secularists with lively and friendly dialogue, and to non-Catholic Christian churches with an open mind and heart. Like his colleague archbishop Karol Wojtyla (later Pope John Paul II) in Poland, König reached out to the Orthodox and Catholic churches of the East and helped to break down ancient barriers between the two historically divided expressions of Christianity.

Perhaps most remarkable was the work König did "behind the scenes" in his native Austria in the early years of the Nazi occupation. He was ordained a priest in 1933, the year that Adolph Hitler took power in neighboring Germany, and by 1938 he was appointed curate at St. Polten's Cathedral. In that diocese, König's primate, like many other religious leaders who feared for themselves, spoke out in favor of the Auschluss, Hitler's annexation and occupation of Austria. König defied his superior and resisted the Nazi-imposed changes in religious education, working underground for years, only narrowing escaping being sent to a concentration camp with other rebels. At the end of the war, he used his wits and courage to defend the nuns of his diocese from the arriving Soviet soldiers who were set on molesting German women wherever they could find them. And finally, after the war, König was one of the first religious leaders to speak out publicly against the remaining Nazi and anti-Semitic influences in Austrian society. He also insisted that his people share moral responsibility for what happened under the Nazi regime. He later recalled: "The Church did not understand early enough that it must urge people to search their consciences. . . . We saw ourselves as victims."[7]

Practices

Selecting a Patron Saint

I T IS NO ACCIDENT THAT CATHOLICS MORE OFTEN have biblical first names than do Protestants. Traditionally, Catholic parents have given their children names of saints and encouraged them to model themselves after the saint's virtuous example. This is first celebrated in the initiation sacrament of baptism. Paragraph 2156 of the Catechism of the Catholic Church reads:

> The sacrament of Baptism is conferred "in the name of the Father and of the Son and of the Holy Spirit." (Matthew 28:19) In Baptism, the Lord's name sanctifies man, and the Christian receives his name in the Church. This can be the name of a saint, that is, of a disciple who has lived a life of exemplary fidelity to the Lord. The patron saint provides a model of charity; we are assured of his intercession. The "baptismal name" can also express a Christian mystery or Christian virtue. Parents, sponsors and the pastor are to see that a name is not given which is foreign to Christian sentiment.

71

Before the Second Vatican Council, children were also urged to choose the name of a patron saint upon confirmation, which usually takes place at the age of thirteen. Confirmation is one of the three sacraments of initiation, preceded by baptism and followed by the Eucharist. (All three sacraments are conferred simultaneously in Eastern-rite Catholic churches today, as it was done in the church of the ancient period.) Confirmation is the time when Catholics become adults in a spiritual sense.

Tradition has it that parents would encourage their children to choose names of saints, rather than those of ancient heroes, athletes (St. John Chrysostom preached a sermon against such names in the early fifth century), other deities, or nonbelievers. Name day (from the Latin phrase *dies natalis*, or "day of birth") then became an annual celebration in the home, more important than a birthday—just as a saint's feast day, usually celebrated on the day of his or her death, the day that he or she was born anew in heaven, is more important that his or her birthday. The confirmand selected a new name to celebrate becoming a new creature in Christ, and once taken, the saint's name was intended to become the child's identity in a deep and meaningful way. It also served to stimulate the child's curiosity in the life of the saint.

Today, when more than two-thirds of Catholic children remain unconfirmed in the church, it might seem that the spiritual practice of choosing a saint as a spiritual guide is too outdated to be meaningful. But it can still be a way of building and maintaining deep relationships that cross the divide between heaven and earth. Many years ago, I chose St. Francis of Assisi as my patron saint. I prayed words like those below, asking him to teach me and guide me in his unique path of following Christ.

You might choose to select a patron saint of your own. As you read about saints and explore their lives you may discover that one saint, or more, seems to speak, as it were, directly to your own life situation.

PRAYER TO A PATRON SAINT

After you have selected a patron saint, or asked a trusted spiritual adviser to select one for you, pray a prayer such as this one.

Good St. _____, please witness to who I want to become, before God. Assist me and intercede for me as I seek to fulfill the promises of heaven in my life. You faced the same challenges that I face now. Your faithfulness will be a model for me on my journey to model Christ.

Pray for me, St. _____. Pray that I will have the courage, creativity, and happiness that comes from living a holy life. Be with me this day and always as I live to understand and love my inheritance as a child of God.

CHAPTER

5

The Blessed Virgin Mary

Jesus Christ is not known as He ought to be
because Mary has been up to this time unknown.

—St. Louis de Montfort (d. 1716)

Dogma and Devotion

DEVOTION TO THE VIRGIN MARY CENTERS ON
her feminine qualities as mother, handmaiden, and
nurturer, but in the life of the church, it is dogma
that really guides how she is understood.

Mary is recognized as an intercessor to her Son, an exemplar
of quiet and simple faith. She is, according to this view, the perfect
woman; and, of course, also according to this view, she is a lifelong celibate, married more to the Holy Spirit than to Joseph. St.
Gregory Thaumaturgus (d. ca. 270) once rhapsodized in a
homily on the Annunciation: "Today the whole circle of the
earth is filled with joy, since the sojourn of the Holy Spirit has
been realized to men."

Tradition has it that Mary, through her intimate relationship with the Holy Spirit—who inspires all divine knowledge—was far more than a receptacle womb. She was chosen by God and then initiated into the divine plan. Again, a quote from that homily by St. Gregory Thaumaturgus:

> You know, O Mary, things kept hidden from the patriarchs and prophets. You have learned, O virgin, things which were kept concealed until now from the angels. You have heard, O purest one, things of which even the choir of inspired men [Scripture writers] was never deemed worthy. Moses, and David, and Isaiah, and Daniel, and all the prophets, prophesied of Him, but the manner they knew not. Yet you alone, O purest virgin, are now made the recipient of things of which all these were kept in ignorance, and you do learn the origin of them. For where the Holy Spirit is, there are all things readily ordered.

Devotion to Mary is intended to bring greater love for her son, as she is always pointing to him. Her pointing to Christ is figurative, in that her role in redemptive history is to show the way to him. However, representations in art throughout the centuries have also shown Mary literally pointing to the baby Jesus on her lap. In this sense, Mary also plays the role of a great prophet. In medieval art, as well as in Catholic religious festivals today throughout the world, you will see images and statues of the "Enthroned Virgin and Child." The Christ child sits on his mother's lap, not sleepily or playfully, as any child might sit on any mother's lap, but with Mary acting as throne for Christ the King. Mary's pose faces straight ahead and is known in Latin as *Sedes Sapientiae*, or "Throne of Wisdom." Mary is the throne for Christ, Wisdom, symbolizing the vital position she holds, then and now, in the life of Christ and for any believer who wants to know Christ more intimately.

Similarly, Mary is commonly regarded as the "Mother of God" (*Theotokos*). This title has its origins in the first centuries of Christianity. The early Church Council of Ephesus approved Mary as Mother of God in 431 CE, and at the same time, it condemned a theologian by the name of Nestorius who had argued that Mary was only mother to the human nature of Christ.

Mary is also seen as the ideal, faithful disciple, or follower, of Christ. As his mother, Mary possesses a faith that is often mixed with sorrow, as when she and Joseph presented Jesus in the temple, and Simeon and Anna foretold the messiahship of the boy; when she, Joseph, and Jesus were forced to flee to Egypt; when Jesus was lost in busy Jerusalem; when she accompanied Jesus on the way to his death at Calvary; when she witnessed the Crucifixion itself; when she helped her son taken down from the cross (a scene immortalized in the Pietàs of Michelangelo and others); and when her son was buried in the tomb. These seven events, described in the Gospels, are in fact known as the seven sorrows of Mary. She is often described, and prayed to, as "Our Lady of Sorrows."

Catholic teaching on the Virgin Mary is called Mariology. As is the case with all church teaching, it has evolved over the centuries, and much of it confuses Catholic laypeople, let alone Protestants. In 1854, for instance, the church proclaimed the Immaculate Conception of Mary. Pope Pius IX defined this as "the doctrine which declares that the most Blessed Virgin Mary, in the first instant of her conception, by a singular grace and privilege of Almighty God, in view of the merits of Jesus Christ, the Savior of the human race, was preserved exempt from all stain of original sin, is a doctrine revealed by God, and therefore must be believed firmly and constantly by all the faithful." There are very fine distinctions at work here. This doctrine does not teach that the Virgin Mary was miraculously conceived. It is not doubted that Mary had a father and a mother (noncanonical gospels named them Joachim and Anne). In order to emphasize the uniqueness of Mary's role in salvation history, the doctrine of the Immaculate Conception of Mary explains that her soul was sanctified by God's grace from the moment she became human. Mary was born of Adam and Eve—as one would say in speaking metaphorically about the Christian doctrine of original sin—but her soul was never actually tainted by the mistakes of our first parents.

In 1950, another pope by the name of Pius—this time it was Pope Pius XII—declared the doctrine of Mary's Assumption to Heaven. This was the first time that the Catholic church officially stated that the mother of Jesus was more than just a saint. Mary's assumption to heaven elevated her above all other saints, giving her a special place in heaven, where her body and soul are believed to have been assumed after physical death but before any corruption of the body was permitted to happen. Four years later, Mary was given the additional title of Queen of Heaven. Mariologists, including Pope John Paul II, often quote from a sermon preached by sixth-century bishop Theoteknos of Palestine, in which he argued for these teachings: "Christ took His immaculate flesh from the immaculate flesh of Mary. And if He prepared a place in heaven for the Apostles, how much more then for His mother? If Enoch and Elijah were translated to heaven, how much more then should Mary, who like the moon in the midst of stars shines and excels among all prophets and Apostles?"

Eastern Orthodox churches assign another special celebration for Mary, called the Solemnity of the Presentation of the Mother of God, a feast day usually celebrated in late November. This honor refers to a legend from the early church that the pre-school-age Mary was presented at the temple in Jerusalem, just as her son later was, and she precociously learned and taught the scholars and priests of the temple, just as her son later did.

These teachings explain why so many people feel special devotion to the Virgin Mary. But do they help us get any closer to understanding the woman—Mary of Nazareth?

LOUIS DE MONTFORT'S PRAYER TO MARY

St. Louis de Montfort is the prophet par excellence of the Virgin Mary in the history of Catholic spirituality (see the brief profile of him on page 58). He dedicated himself to rekindling devotion to the Mother of God in the early eighteenth century, and he often used the most extravagant images and phrases to describe this devotion. He was also effusive in his praise of Mary as an archetype for our lives and as a mediator to her son.

Most Protestants will likely be uncomfortable with some of Montfort's phrasings in the prayer that follows (particularly in paragraph 1), as he prays to Mary with language that seems to only rightly belong to God in Christ. Paragraphs two and three, on the other hand, are lovely examples of devotion to and respect for Mary as the ideal Christian.

Paragraph One

Hail Mary, beloved Daughter of the Eternal Father! Hail Mary, admirable Mother of the Son! Hail Mary, faithful spouse of the Holy Ghost! Hail Mary, my dear Mother, my loving Mistress, my powerful sovereign! Hail my joy, my glory, my heart and my soul! Thou art all mine by mercy, and I am all thine by justice. But I am not yet sufficiently thine. I now give myself wholly to thee without keeping anything back for myself or others. If thou still seest in me anything which does not belong to thee, I beseech thee to take it and to make thyself the absolute Mistress of all that is mine. Destroy in me all that may be displeasing to God, root it up and bring it to nought; place and cultivate in me everything that is pleasing to thee.

Paragraph Two

May the light of thy faith dispel the darkness of my mind; may thy profound humility take the place of my pride; may thy sublime contemplation check the distractions of my wandering imagination; may thy continuous sight of God fill my memory with His presence; may the burning love of thy heart inflame the lukewarmness of mine; may thy virtues take the place of my sins; may thy merits be my only adornment in the sight of God and make up for all that is wanting in me. Finally, dearly beloved Mother, grant, if it be possible, that I may have no other spirit but thine to know Jesus and His divine will; that I may have no other soul but thine to praise and glorify the Lord; that I may have no other heart but thine to love God with a love that is pure and ardent. I do not ask thee for visions, revelations, sensible devotion or spiritual pleasures. It is thy privilege to see God clearly; it is thy privilege to enjoy heavenly bliss; it is thy privilege to triumph gloriously in Heaven at the right hand of thy Son and to hold absolute sway over angels, men and demons; it is thy privilege to dispose of all the gifts of God, just as thou willest.

Paragraph Three

Such is, O heavenly Mary, the "best part," which the Lord has given thee and which shall never be taken away from thee—and this thought fills my heart with joy. As for my part here below, I wish for no other than that which was thine: to believe sincerely without spiritual pleasures; to suffer joyfully without human consolation; to die continually to myself without respite; and to work zealously and unselfishly for thee until death as the humblest of thy servants. The only grace I beg thee to obtain for me is that every day and every moment of my life I may say: Amen, so be it—to all that thou didst do while on earth; Amen, so be it—to all that thou art now doing in Heaven; Amen, so be it—to all that thou art doing in my soul, so that thou alone mayest fully glorify Jesus in me for time and eternity. Amen.

Relating to Mary of Nazareth Today

MANY A PROTESTANT WANTING TO BETTER UNDERSTAND Catholic spirituality has stumbled over the idealization of Mary. Those very real moments of faith in Mary's life are blurred by the saccharine piety that is so often imaged in her. Like an Albrecht Dürer engraving, the idealized Mary is one-dimensional and fails to capture much that would allow us to relate to: her cascading fair hair curls over her delicate shoulders as she looks placidly at the boy who will later bring her fame and devotion.

The physical descriptions we might form of Mary based on depictions in European art of the Virgin would have little or no relationship to the actual woman, Mary of Nazareth, according to most scholars today. The following description summarizes the most recent scholarship:

> She is thirteen. Short and wiry, with dark olive skin. The trace of a mustache on her upper lip, soft black down on her arms and legs. The muscles are hard knots in her arms, solid lines in her calves.
>
> Her hair is almost black, and has been folded into a single braid down her back for as long as she can remember. The weight of it raises her chin and makes her walk tall, as she has learned to do when carrying jars of water or bundles of kindling on her head. You don't bend under the burden. You root into the ground and grow out of it, reaching up and becoming taller. The greater the weight, the taller you become: the peasant woman's secret of making the burden light.[1]

Even the pregnant belly of Mary, growing with Jesus inside of her, is nearly impossible to find in the first sixteen centuries of Christian art and storytelling.

The New Testament would seem to offer a full picture of Mary, but we actually know very little about her from its pages. The apostle Paul never mentions Mary by name in any of his letters. No contemporary of hers ever wrote a life or gospel about her. Why is the real Mary so shrouded in mystery?

Elizabeth, another great early New Testament woman of faith (she was the mother of John the Baptist), was the first to say to her friend and cousin, "Blessed are you among women, and blessed is the fruit of your womb." And Mary agreed: "Surely, from now on all generations will call me blessed;" she said, as her soul magnified the Lord in her pregnancy (Luke 1:42, 48).

Are Protestants equally enjoined to call Mary "blessed"? Many of the traditional descriptions of Mary encompass her special spiritual roles as intercessor, joy for the suffering, and she who knows the way. These are images of the Mother of God that speak closely to me. But why is Mary able to intercede for us in special ways? What is it about this woman in particular that enables her to specially minister to those in need?

Mary showed a mother's faith in her son, Jesus, as well as a sinner's faith in Christ. At the wedding at Cana, where Jesus performed his first miracle recorded in John's Gospel, it was Mary who showed both aspects of confidence in who he was. "Do whatever he tells you," (John 2:5) she said to the servants, knowing better than anyone else what her grown son would do, and who he would become.

She was the first and the greatest of the disciples. She was the one who bore Christ in her womb and, later, bore Christ in her soul. Mary was close to her son, Jesus. She had the sort of understanding that comes through emotion and passion rather than facts and evidence, a mother's understanding of her child—which was unavailable to even the twelve apostles.

She also knew sadness, oppression, terror, rejection, and hard work. Joan Chittister, a Benedictine nun and popular conference speaker, recently wrote the following words—which have gotten her into trouble with many traditional Catholics—in a booklet titled *Mary, Wellspring of Peace: A Contemporary Novena:*

> A close reading of scripture reveals a woman immersed in the same pressing issues that echo in our times. Mary was unwed and pregnant, an advocate for the oppressed, a political refugee, a single parent, a mother of a condemned prisoner, a Third World woman, a liberator, a widow, the first disciple.

These images of Mary are surely new to most of us—but they are true. They help uncover the Mary of Nazareth who speaks to our world today, as opposed to the idealized Mary who seems to be more of an ever-faithful, perpetual-virgin mirage dreamed up by men than a real person. The Mary of history stands for freedom and justice as much as for quiet faith.

Finally, Mary said yes to God just as we hope to do. Her voice rings out through history as the perfect example of joy and acceptance of God's will, not just submission to it, that comes from knowing oneself and one's God. Mary said, "Here am I, the servant of the Lord; let it be with me according to your word" (Luke 1:38). When we look more closely at Mary, we see more of the real woman, and we see in her the difference between being a saint and just being saintly.[2]

Spiritual Practice with the Blessed Virgin Mary

MARY CUTS TO THE ROOT OF THE SEPARATION OF PROTESTANT from Catholic. While the average Catholic desires to know mysticism for him- or herself in some way, the average Protestant distrusts it. Mary is the dividing line, and until we come to understand her for who she really is, we will be separated from one of the most important avenues to knowing God in Christ.

We can become like Mary, too, asking for her help and intercession along the way. She is a teacher, a companion, and an intercessor whom any Christian should want to have in his or her corner. It is okay, even for a Protestant, to ask for Mary's help.

The apostle Paul wrote letters to the first churches in Rome, Corinth, Ephesus, and Colossae, asking the believers there to pray to God on his behalf. This was an innovation of Paul that stood in contrast to the Judaism from which he grew; the community of saints, both on earth and in heaven, may speak to God and petition God on our behalf.

Paul said to the people in Rome: "[J]oin me in earnest prayer to God on my behalf" (Romans 15:30). He said to the people in Corinth: "[J]oin in helping us by your prayers, so that many will give thanks on our behalf for the blessing granted us through the prayers of many" (2 Corinthians 1:11). To the Ephesians, he wrote: "Pray in the Spirit at all times in every prayer and supplication. To that end keep alert and always persevere in supplication for all the saints" (Ephesians 6:18). And to the church at Colossae, he said: "Devote yourselves to prayer, keeping alert in it with thanksgiving. At the same time pray for us as well" (Colossians 4:2-3).

In that same spirit, we can say, "Mary, pray for us."

THE SONG OF MARY

The most popular prayer of the New Testament, after Christ's teaching of the Lord's Prayer to the disciples, is the Song of Mary, the Magnificat (Luke 1:46–55). We can pray with Mary today and model not just her quiet yes to God but also her hope and compassion for all in need.

> My soul magnifies the Lord,
>> and my spirit rejoices in God my Savior,
> for he has looked with favor on the lowliness of his servant.
>> Surely, from now on all generations will call me
>> blessed;
> for the Mighty One has done great things for me,
>> and holy is his name.

His mercy is for those who fear him
   from generation to generation.
He has shown strength with his arm;
   he has scattered the proud in the thoughts of
   their hearts.
He has brought down the powerful from their thrones,
   and lifted up the lowly;
he has filled the hungry with good things,
   and sent the rich away empty.
He has helped his servant Israel,
   in remembrance of his mercy,
according to the promise he made to our ancestors,
   to Abraham and to his descendants forever.

As we pray with Mary, may we be pregnant with love of
God and our neighbor.

PRAYER TO OUR LADY
OF FIFTH AVENUE

The following prayer accompanies the statue of Mary and
the child Jesus that was dedicated at St. Thomas (Episcopal)
Church on Fifth Avenue in New York City in 1991. The statue
is approximately four feet tall. It was created by a Benedictine
nun, Mother Concordia Scott, and given by the parish to mark
the fifteenth anniversary of their rector. The prayer includes
theological subtleties that will put many Protestants at ease.

I come to you, Holy Mother,
to ask your prayers for _____.

You give us all encouragement to approach you
as your children, whose brother, your son
Jesus Christ, we claim as our blessed Savior
and yours.

Help me now, I ask you, with a prayer
to Him on my behalf and for His sake.
Amen.

Practices

Sr. Rosemarie Greco, D.W.

S
R. ROSEMARIE GRECO IS THE DIRECTOR OF WISDOM
House Retreat and Conference Center in Litchfield,
Connecticut, an ecumenical retreat center that provides a
contemplative environment for meditation, prayer, and spiritual
growth. She is a member of the Daughters of Wisdom community
of nuns (hence the D.W. after her name), a scholar, a popular
retreat leader, and a spiritual teacher.

Ever since I was a child, I knew the friendship of saints.
Growing up Roman Catholic in a family with a wonderful
Italian heritage, educated in Catholic schools, I considered
the saints part of my family. The saints were "friends of
God" and people who knew the joys and struggles of
everyday life. They were people who kept faithful to God
amid difficulties, and because of their commitment to
God—and sometimes because of their determination in the

87

midst of struggle—they endured. They were recognized by their friends as having stood for something.

We wanted to know more about them and drew near to them. Sometimes this "drawing near" was in order to ask a favor, such as calling upon St. Anthony to help us find something. At other times, the "drawing near" to them was something like going to a mentor or friend who would help us live our lives in some type of imitation of them.

As a schoolgirl, I remember liking St. Thérèse of Lisieux: her life in a Carmelite cloister was attractive to me, and I wanted to develop a spirituality similar to hers. As I grew older, I came to know many other saints in the Christian family, but only in the past ten years have I come to know one who is a Daughter of Wisdom.

The Daughters of Wisdom are a congregation of women religious (sometimes called nuns). We were founded in France in 1703 by St. Louis de Montfort and Blessed Marie Louise Trichet. I have a newfound friendship with Blessed Marie Louise Trichet.

Although not formally canonized by the Roman Catholic church, as St. Louis de Montfort is, she is a woman with growing influence in my life. She is acclaimed by many for her holiness, even though her full recognition by the church is still in process. Only in the past decade or so have some of her letters and experiences become accessible to many. I was excited when I discovered one of her inspirational words, which says, "If I were a piece of cloth, I would give myself to the poor." Those words, spoken during a time of famine in France, seemed to capture the way God, divine wisdom, became manifest in her. They became a challenge to me as well, asking for my commitment to those who are poor.

Since 1990, I have been the director of Wisdom House Retreat and Conference Center in Litchfield, Connecticut. It was in this position that I came to know Marie Louise in another way. I discovered that she had been the administrator and finance manager of the "Poor House" in Poitiers, France. She had no funds and had to provide basic food, clothing, and shelter to not only the residents of the Poor House but also to her community of sisters. I was able to identify with this reality and began to pray to her for guidance, insight, and wisdom for my own situation at Wisdom House. I went to her as a mentor and needed to learn from her, even if the learning was to "live by faith."

In 1997, I commissioned an icon of Blessed Marie Louise. A generous donor provided funds, and iconographer Angela Manno of New York wrote the icon. I have sat before this icon many times filled with discouragement, other times with anger, demanding that she do something to alleviate the burden of my difficult situation as administrator. "I was trained in theology, not in financial management!" I would say.

There were no immediate results, but there were results that were gradual and took patience, persistence, and faith to recognize them. A few months ago, I was given an outline of a presentation that spoke about Marie Louise Trichet and the spirituality of financial management. I came across this statement about her, which really resonated with me: "A businesswoman by necessity rather than by choice, several new foundations found her confronting administrators and sometimes even bishops, contract in hand, battling to save the original nature of an apostolic congregation of universal dimensions." This did it for me. I could identify with these words about Marie Louise, and I felt comforted and confirmed in the continuing challenge of blending administration with theology, finance with spirituality.

Then my family came into perspective. I remembered that my grandmothers and grandfathers all had a hand in clothing, food, and construction businesses. They all had an eye out for those who did not have enough food, clothing, or shelter, and they gave freely. My parents continued in this vein. When I realized, through coming to know Blessed Marie Louise, that I had been prepared for this work all along, it was an "aha moment."

Blessed Marie Louise is one saint whose advice I seek these days. She knows the life of an administrator and organizer. She knows what it means to have a vision and to depend on others for the means to make the vision come about. She is a friend of God, a patron of administrators and finance managers, and a friend of the poor—just as I try to be.

PART TWO

Doubt, Mystery, and Faith

AFTER THE LAST WAR, EVERYONE WAS TALKING about the lost generation. After this war, thank God, they are talking more about saints. . . .

A few years ago there was a book review in the *New York Times* about . . . Moby Dick as an allegorical novel. . . . W. H. Auden was the author of the review . . . and he writes, "There is the possibility of each becoming exceptional and good; this ultimate possibility for hero and chorus alike is stated in Father Mapple's sermon, and it is to become a saint, i.e., the individual through his own free will surrenders his will to the will of God. In this surrender he does not become the ventriloquist's doll, for the God who acts through him can only do so by his consent; there always remain two wills, and the saint therefore never ceases to be tempted to obey his own desires. The saint does not ask to become one, he is called to become one and assents to the call."

Doubt, Mystery, and Faith

The choice . . . is not between good and evil . . . but between good and better.

—Dorothy Day, quoting W. H. Auden[1]

The Making of a Saint:
How Is It Done Today?

WE HAVE SEEN THE NATURAL EVOLUTION OF how heroes of the faith were originally set apart in the early church as martyrs and saints. Eventually, in the tenth century, the making of saints was normalized, and the power to do it was consolidated in Rome with the pope. Procedures and expectations for canonization were really codified in the century after the Protestant Reformation, and the method that was established in 1634 is basically the same method in force today.

The *Catechism of the Catholic Church* explains in paragraph 828:

> By canonizing some of the faithful, i.e., by solemnly proclaiming that they practiced heroic virtue and lived in fidelity to God's grace, the Church recognizes the power of the Spirit of holiness within her and sustains the hope of believers by proposing the saints to them as models and intercessors. "The saints have always been the source and origin of renewal in the most difficult moments in the Church's history." (John Paul II)

But how exactly is a saint made? There are three major steps in the process of making a saint in the Roman Catholic church: the opening of a formal case, beatification, and canonization.

Since the tenth century, there has always been a waiting period before a person's case for sainthood can be opened, but the duration has differed from era to era. Until 1917, the customary waiting period before opening a case was fifty years after the person's death—so long that those who had known the subject would also likely be dead. The waiting period was seen as a way to lend objectivity to a process that had, in the early church, been based primarily on popular opinion.

Nevertheless, on several occasions a pope has accelerated the cause of a saint because of a personal relationship he had with the person. Perhaps most famously, Francis of Assisi's special counselor, Cardinal Ugolino, who was elected Pope Gregory IX just after the little poor man's death, presided over Francis's rapid canonization only two years later. Another rapid canonization that was known throughout Europe was that of Thomas à Becket in 1173, less than three years after his martyrdom in the cathedral at Canterbury. In that case, Pope Alexander III, Becket's friend and confidant during the latter's many conflicts with King Henry II, oversaw a quick canonization to satisfy the people of England and Europe, as well as the millions of pilgrims who had already made Canterbury a principal place for pilgrimage—even though it alienated the sovereign of Becket's own country and many of the priests and bishops there who sought to remain in favor with the king who had once wanted Becket's death. Only one year after Becket's canonization, the guilty king made his own pilgrimage to the shrine of the saint he had had murdered. More recently, Pope John Paul II has sped along the process for Mother Teresa, his friend and contemporary. We will look more closely at her case later in this chapter.

Today, the customary waiting period before the process may officially begin is five years after the death of the faithful one. The process begins with the pope receiving recommendations for possible beatifications from local dioceses. An appointed team of diocesan leaders and Vatican officials then investigates the life of the proposed candidate, reviewing recommendations for the opening of a case, in a process that resembles the preparing of legal briefs. The formal opening of a case is the first step toward sainthood. Ultimately, the pope makes the decision to open a case, which means that further arguments will be heard for the cause.

For example, the case of Mother Marianne Cope of Molokai (Hawaii) was formally opened when Pope John Paul II decreed on April 19, 2004, that her heroic virtue had been confirmed. The German-born Cope (b. 1838) joined the Sisters of St. Francis as a young woman. She worked for most of her life with leprosy patients in Hawaii, and her cause for sainthood is being championed by dioceses on the Pacific Islands, where she is buried, and in Syracuse, New York, where the Sisters of St. Francis are headquartered. Her case is now under way.

The second step for Mother Marianne—or for any potential saint—is beatification. This process involves the gathering, reviewing, and authenticating of miracles attributed to the person under consideration. In Mother Marianne's case, one miracle is already waiting to be attested, which would lead to her official beatification. These miracles are usually healings that come after a devotee has prayed for the intercession of the candidate. In addition to attesting a miracle claim, at this stage Vatican authorities will hear testimonies from witnesses both for and against the candidate, examine the subject's writings for orthodoxy, and eventually discern whether or not miracles occurred as a result of the candidate's intercession after death or, sometimes, during life. In this last regard, the making of saints remains a somewhat democratic process even today. Just as popular devotion turned the dead into saints in the earliest centuries of the church, when people today begin to pray to a potential saint or otherwise show devotion or respect for his or her life and ministry on earth, it fuels the canonization process. These popular movements are very much like grass roots political campaigns, as people advocate for their candidate and offer prayers to him or her. Popes do the same, as when John Paul II prayed to Edith Stein, also known as Teresa Benedicta of the Cross, at Auschwitz in 1979 just after his election as pope and almost twenty years before he canonized her. It is this "campaigning" that not only summons the attention of church authorities but also makes it possible to accumulate evidence that the candidate has indeed helped in the answering of prayers.

The church distinguishes between martyrs and confessors when considering candidates for beatification. Martyrs have paid the ultimate price for their faith, and their sanctity is not in question. No proven miracles are required, in fact, for a martyr's beatification; it is assumed that they are in heaven receiving their reward. Confessors, on the other hand, are candidates whose holiness must be verified; their beatification and canonization are only possible through the attesting of miracles.[1]

Canonization is the third step in the process. It includes something very practical for believers: a declaration that the canonized is certainly with God in heaven. In other words, a saint is known with certainty to be available for prayer and assistance. This is what the devoted author of a letter written about the death of Venerable Bede (d. 735) meant when he recounted Bede's last moments:

> [S]inging "Glory be to the Father and to the Son and to the Holy Spirit" and the rest, he breathed his last. And well may we believe without hesitation that, inasmuch as he had laboured here always in the praise of God, so his soul was carried by angels to the joys of Heaven which he longed for.[2]

Thérèse of Lisieux (d. 1897) had the quickest canonization in the modern era (and she may be surpassed by Mother Teresa of Calcutta, who was beatified in short order in 2003 and may soon be canonized). Thérèse was declared a saint in 1925, only twenty-eight years after her death.

"The Little Flower," as she was called, was only twenty-four years old when she died. She barely had time to learn to care for herself as an adult before she died and became a granter of miracles to those who prayed to her. Her sweetness and innocence reminded her contemporaries—the millions who read her autobiography soon after her death—of the Virgin Mary. Especially to the late-Victorian mind-set, Thérèse's youth, kindness, and full face were reminiscent of the Mother of Jesus. But in a youthful and modern style, Thérèse eschewed mystical experiences as unnecessary for holiness and argued that righteousness is for all people, secular and religious. One recent biographer explains the impact that she had on the early twentieth century:

> By 1915, nearly a million copies [of her autobiography, *The Story of a Soul*] were in print; a separate publication anthologized the hundreds of thousands of letters (arriving at a rate of five hundred a day, one thousand a day by 1925) that bore witness to miracles granted by Thérèse's intercession.[3]

The faithful have credited Thérèse with thousands of miracles over the last hundred years, but two had to be verified in order for her to be beatified, and another two verified miracles would open the door for her canonization. In the end, three of the miracles were healings from tuberculosis, the disease that took Thérèse's own life, and the fourth was the healing of a nun from a deadly ulcer. Many today who pray to Thérèse to intercede for them claim to experience the smell of sweet flowers when in the real presence of the Little Flower.

When Mother Teresa of Calcutta was beatified, it was also a rapid process in response to popular demand. Pope John Paul II, who knew Mother Teresa personally and championed her causes throughout his life, granted a special dispensation to open her case only two years after her death. Today, at least two posthumous miracles must be demonstrated and attributed to the intervention of the person in order to declare her a saint worthy of veneration. In Mother Teresa's case, when one miracle had been documented—the healing of a sick woman in India who had prayed to her—Teresa was cleared for beatification, which was celebrated in Rome in 2003. Canonization is sure to follow soon, but a second miracle will need to be documented before that can officially happen.

THE TROUBLE WITH POSTHUMOUS MIRACLES

In talking about the canonization of saints, it is necessary to highlight one important distinction. Some saints are canonized for their work on earth, and some are canonized for their "work" after death. Mother Teresa is a recent prime example of the first category. Like Francis of Assisi before her, Mother Teresa lived such an obviously saintly life, completely for other people and for God, that if she had lived during the first centuries of Christianity she would have been venerated as a saint immediately upon her death. In the modern context of her death, the church still rushed to canonize her, and on Sunday, October 19, 2003, more than 300,000 people crowded into St. Peter's Square in Vatican City to hear John Paul II announce that important second step in the process, beatifying the small Albanian woman. "Brothers and sisters," John Paul said to the crowd, "even in our days God inspires new models of sainthood. Some impose themselves for their radicalness, like that offered by Mother Teresa of Calcutta."

In contrast to Mother Teresa—who lived a saintly life—are other saints who become known only after their deaths. These figures seem to owe as much of their popularity to the earnestness of their followers to find something to believe in as they do to real presences of sanctity. St. Foy (third century)—a child martyr from the Roman era—is one such saint. Her relics have drawn pilgrims to a remote monastery in Conques, France, for centuries. The reliquary that holds her bones is made of gold and studded with jewels, a masterpiece of Gothic art that is carefully protected today. Her posthumous deeds and healing powers have inspired poets. The cult of St. Foy has centered exclusively on the power of this child saint to perform miracles after her death. At times, Foy has performed these miracles "in person," as a spirit would enter into the natural world in order to help someone in need. Such occasions, as recorded in the late-medieval text *The Book of Miracles of Sainte Foy,* include the restoration of a man's eyes after they had been torn from his head, the reviving of a mule from death, the murder of a man who was slandering Foy, and the freeing of a man bound for hanging—and the list goes on and on.

Also chronicled in this amazing document are those miracles that reinforced St. Foy's shrine as a place for pilgrims to donate their heirlooms of gold and jewels. Conques is located in the south of France on one of the ancient roads that lead through northern Spain to the popular medieval pilgrimage destination of Compostela. Compostela was once second only to Jerusalem as a pilgrimage destination during the Middle Ages. Conques is also near several crossroads taken by soldiers who were coming from and going to battles during the Crusades. Pilgrims and Crusaders would ask for Foy's protection and guidance, rewarding her for her kindnesses upon their return. These instances of wonderwork show us a side to medieval devotion that was either scripted by the corrupt in the church at that time or, at least, gladly tolerated.

Another unfortunate practice inherited from the Middle Ages is the recruitment of saints for protection in battle and help for victory. In the ninth century, for instance, Alfonso the Great sought St. Anthony's help in heaven for winning land back from the Moors, Muslim invaders who occupied much of Europe during the Middle Ages. Victory came. One century earlier, Charlemagne had conquered some lands of the Moors in Spain after being prodded by three visions from St. James, in which the apostle promised heavenly aid to the cause. It was the spoils of war, in fact, that funded the construction of the remarkable cathedral at Santiago de Compostela, which translates as "St. James of Compostela." A history could be written of the saints who have aided Christians in defeating the Moors.

Plenty of saints showed themselves remarkable in life so as to make it unnecessary to also focus attention on those who only seem to cast miracles like spells after their death.

CONTROVERSIAL SAINTS

When a cause for sainthood has been officially assigned to one of the priests of the Congregation for the Causes of Saints in Rome, the canon lawyers become involved. A defense lawyer prepares the brief that demonstrates the case for official sanctity, and a sort of prosecutor, called the promoter of the faith—or, colloquially, the devil's advocate—prepares objections to and arguments against the case. Sometimes, the arguments of the devil's advocate are not adequately satisfied, and the case stalls somewhere in the Vatican. Even when cases do proceed, they are occasionally subject to later review or revision.

Anyone who attended Catholic school in the 1940s or 1950s will tell you that he or she used to know the calendar of saints by heart, before it was changed after the Second Vatican Council. On occasion, dubious saints have been officially dropped from the Roman Catholic calendar. When serious doubts are raised about the historical accuracy of the accounts of a saint's life, for instance, investigations are reopened, and it is possible that the saint will be removed from the approved list for veneration. This happened in systematic fashion in 1969, when Pope Paul VI reorganized the liturgical year and revised the calendar of saints.

Chief among the demoted saints in history is Catherine of Alexandria, whose famous legend left us with the term *Catherine wheel,* the instrument of her torture. It was said that after Catherine was finally beheaded, her body was carried to Mount Sinai by angels. To this day, one of the most important monasteries in Christendom, located on Mount Sinai and which became a place of refuge for monks and icons throughout the iconoclastic wars and world wars that have plagued Europe, is named for her. The Holy Monastery of St. Catherine is, in fact, the oldest inhabited monastery in the world. The Greek and Russian Orthodox churches commemorate her today, as does the Church of England (Anglican/Episcopal), but Rome dropped her from the Catholic liturgical calendar in 1969. In addition to Catherine, St. Ursula, St. Philomena, St. Nicholas, and eighty-nine others were also dropped at that time.

Sometimes the veneration of a saint is so great that it feeds the legend despite historical doubts. Or it could be that, for many, the relationship one has with a saint has little to do with faith in historical verifiability and more to do with faith that the sort of things we see in saints' lives are possible with God. This is another example of how believing in the saints and making them a part of our lives and consciousness is one with our belief in God and what God can do.

John Paul II became pontiff in 1978 and has been the longest-reigning pope since Pius IX, who served from 1846 to 1878. At this writing, John Paul II appears to be in the last months of his papacy due to the effects of Parkinson's disease. In the twenty-five-plus years of his reign, he has canonized and beatified more men and women than all the previous pontiffs combined: more than 1,300 altogether, or more than fifty each year—equal to one for each week of his papacy. His extraordinary interest in multiplying saints has gone largely unnoticed by the average Catholic, except on those occasions when the honored subject's sanctity is not universally recognized.

100

For example, we have Pope Pius IX. On the same day that John Paul II beatified Pope John XXIII, the lovable Italian who championed the reforms of Vatican II, he also beatified Pius IX (on September 3, 2000). Pius, who is often referred to as Pio Nono in Italy, is most infamously remembered for what came to be known as "the kidnapping of Edgardo Mortara," in which a Jewish boy was removed from his family and baptized a Catholic against the family's will. Pius IX is also a controversial figure among the ecumenical community, as he oversaw the assignment of papal infallibility as dogma, making belief in it a requirement for true Catholic faith. His interest in centralizing power in the papacy was so great, in fact, that when one of his theologians contested the new doctrine on the grounds of tradition, Pius IX responded angrily, "*I am Tradition.*"[4] He was also the author of an encyclical titled *A Syllabus of Errors,* in which he condemned the principles of democratic, liberal thinking that define much of modern society today—for example, a free press, freedom of conscience, civil rights, and the separation of church and state.

Many people, particularly leaders in the Jewish community, also protested the canonization of Edith Stein. Teresa Benedicta of the Cross, as she renamed herself upon entering a Carmelite convent in Cologne in 1933, was born Jewish and converted to Christianity after reading the autobiography of Teresa of Avila. She took her final vows in 1938, just four years before she was deported to the Auschwitz concentration camp and murdered by the Nazis. She converted to Catholicism at a time when the church's Good Friday liturgy still contained anti-Semitic language (it was removed during Vatican II reforms). Edith Stein, or Teresa Benedicta of the Cross, expressed what Jewish leaders regard as anti-Semitism when she wrote in her final will that she hoped to be martyred as a Jew in order to help atone for the lack of faith in her people. She was beatified in 1987 and canonized in 1998.

Practices

M. Basil Pennington, O.C.S.O.

M. BASIL PENNINGTON, O.C.S.O., HAS BEEN A Cistercian monk for more than fifty years and is a popular author of many books on centering prayer, *lectio divina,* and other subjects. He has led a fascinating life as a religious and even in world events. Pennington was present at the Second Vatican Council, and he was the first Western monk to make an extended stay on Mount Athos. A cofounder of the centering prayer movement, he was a friend of Thomas Merton and many other current and future saints.

One of the great consolations of our faith is that when our loved ones leave us, born to eternal life, they find a home among the saints. So first of all I have a personal relationship with my parents, my brother, my grandparents, my aunts and uncles, and a couple of nephews, and also with the members of my monastic communities who have gone ahead, with my mentors and spiritual fathers, and with those who were my friends in this life.

103

Those among the saints to whom I feel especially close are Mother Teresa, Pope John XXIII, Frank Duff, Patrick Peyton, and Fulton Sheen, for they are friends I knew here.

I was given certain patron saints in baptism, Robert Bellarmine and John the Beloved, and I have cultivated relationships with them. I adopted others: John Vianney, Robert of Newminister, and Robert of Molesmes, the founder of Cîteaux; along with the other Cistercian founders: Alberic, Stephen Harding, the Cistercian fathers, and, of course, Benedict of Nursia, who wrote our Rule. I spent some time with the Salesians and got to know Don Bosco, their founder, as a friend. Aloysius is special: I chose him at confirmation, and he was given to me as a novice. But most special is my monastic patron, Basil the Great, along with Basil the Fool.

For some reason I became aware of a couple of saints early on and undertook to pray for their canonizations— Maximilian Kolbe and Josephine Bakhita—and have had the joy of seeing them canonized.

I have a special devotion to St. Anne. During the Holy Year of 1950, I wanted to go on pilgrimage; I was seeking to discern my vocation. Being poor, I could not go abroad, so I got three friends to drive to Beaupre with me. When we arrived there and on our return trip I received many clear indications in regard to my vocation, and an obstacle was removed while I was on pilgrimage. By coincidental circumstances, the abbot decided I should make my first profession on St. Anne's feast and later that I should be consecrated a monk on her most important day, the birthday of her daughter, Mary. Still later, prior to my election, the community decided that their new abbot should be blessed on that feast. When Spencer Abbey was built, a statue of St. Anne was placed in the garth. The monks believe this statue miraculously prevented a fire that devastated most of the old abbey from harming the infirmary. When the new church was built, the altar in the transept, opposite St. Joseph's, was dedicated in honor of St. Anne. I pass it several times a day. On the day of my profession, Abbot Edmund told me to ask St. Anne to help me remain faithful to the interior life and a life a prayer. Each time I pass this altar, that is my prayer.

St. Joseph is also a very special person in my life. He was the patron my saintly father took when he was baptized in the Catholic church. We count on St. Joseph to watch over us as he watched over Jesus and Mary and to watch over this abbey as he watched over the home in Nazareth.

Some refer to the Mother of Jesus, the Blessed Virgin Mary, Our Lady, as St. Mary, but I think we Catholics generally think of her as apart from the saints. Theologically we speak of her receiving an honor and devotion above that of all the other saints and their receiving their grace in some way through her as the queen of heaven and earth. At a very early age I learned to pray the rosary, and since then it has hardly ever been absent from my life. It is usually in my pocket, where I can grasp it and pray some Ave's whenever I have a free moment. It is sort of a tangible link to Mary and heaven.

Another link is the medal I wear around my neck. It is called the Miraculous Medal because the Lord worked so many miracles through it. Mary appeared to Catherine Labouré at the convent on the Rue de Bac in 1830 and asked her to have this medal made. I don't wear it in expectation of miracles but to honor the Lady in my life.

The scapular was originally the "sweater" the monks would put on when they took off their cowls to go to work. In 1272, Mary gave Simon Stock a scapular to wear as a sign of her protection. The scapular took on this meaning and began to be worn by all religious and even lay folk. Because it was not possible to wear the ample scapular all the time, a medal was designed that could be worn as a substitute for the scapular. Although I wear the scapular much of the time in the monastery, I also wear the scapular medal all the time, looking for Mary's care and protection.

When I became a monk it was the practice in our order for all to receive the name of Mary as well as a saint's name. That practice has been largely discontinued, but I keep the M. in honor of Mary and to signify that I belong to her. In 1951 I read St. Louis de Montfort's *True Devotion,* and, inspired by that, on January 31 of that year I dedicated my life to Mary and her service in service of her son, Jesus. Within five months I was in her abbey, the Abbey of Blessed Mary of St. Joseph. ("Mary of Joseph" was what Mary was called in her lifetime.) According to Cistercian practice, there is a shrine of Mary at the door of the church, and as we enter and leave we always send at least a little prayer in her direction.

I have also written some books in honor of Mary and included a chapter on her in others. Our relationship is so close that to say that it is that of a mother and son does not seem sufficient. Each night we end our day by singing the "Salve Regina": "Hail, holy Queen, Mother of mercy, our life, our sweetness and our hope . . . most gracious advocate . . . O clement, O loving, O sweet Virgin Mary."

Living largely according to the church calendar, we honor Mary and all these other saints through the year on the different liturgical feasts. At other times I become aware of their presence for one reason or another and ask them to pray for us.

In my room I have an icon of Mary, which was painted for me by one of the monks; another combined icon of Mary and Basil, carved by a monk of Mount Athos for me at the request of Archimandrite Aimilianos; and another icon of St. Basil, painted for me by one of our Irish nuns. In my office I have a picture of Mary, painted for me by Br. Alberic on the occasion of my abbatial blessing, and a drawing of Mary, given to me by a friend before she died. It had been done for her by a friend dying of AIDS. Both pictures are very tender. When I look upon these images I always breathe at least a quick prayer, but at times they draw me deeply. I often enclose in my letters a small picture of Mary, sometimes the one printed to commemorate my ordination to the priesthood or my abbatial blessing.

I have spent many hours reading the writings of my heavenly friends, letting them speak to me from their hearts to my heart. Besides the inspired authors of the sacred

Scriptures, those who have especially nourished me are an early Cistercian, Bernard of Clairvaux; the other Cistercian fathers; Columba Marmion (as I mentioned); Thomas Aquinas; Thomas Merton; and Pierre Teilhard de Chardin.

I believe all these friends in heaven, in some way in the Lord, are able to maintain a caring watch on my life and in their great purity and freedom are able to intercede most effectively for me with the Lord. When Jesus made us his friend he made us all friends. I look forward to heaven, when we will be able to enjoy one another totally and forever.

The Radical Triumph of
the Protestant Idea

I T IS IMPOSSIBLE TO COMPREHEND MEDIEVAL FEELINGS about saints and their value without first understanding the medieval belief in purgatory. Today's Catholic church still teaches purgatory, but the faithful do not believe in it as intensely as they did in the days of Hieronymus Bosch, Dante, and their vivid images of what might actually happen there. We don't live as intimately with God as our foremothers and forefathers did, and the fear of God is not the great motivator that it once was, even though our prayers still resound with the themes that fueled the medieval fear of God that we avoid. Today, we more commonly believe in God in ways that remove divine causes and effects from our lives. Our theologies and cosmologies often diminish God's power. The language of our prayers in church on Saturday or Sunday no longer matches our intellectual beliefs about God's power and influence throughout the week. We experience neither the threats nor the blessings of God, as was possible when God was the dominant and most intimate effect on human life.

Until relatively recently (the last few generations), most
Christians believed in the active and deliberate power of God to
damn and pardon. Hell, purgatory, heaven, evil spirits, good
spirits—all of these once-vivid things are now lost to most of us.
T. S. Eliot wrote: "The glory of man is his capacity for salvation;
it is also true to say that his glory is his capacity for damnation."
The French poet Baudelaire once said, "To believe in God you
must also believe in the Devil." Given our relative lack of religious
belief today, perhaps there also isn't much potential glory in
store for us. Our ability or inability to believe in saints—
examples of great goodness—may be in direct proportion to
our ability or inability to believe in supernatural evil.

We feel the question of eternity much less intensely than did
our medieval foremothers and forefathers. Our beliefs have
changed—or our ability to believe has weakened—but also our
need to believe is completely different from the need felt by
earlier generations. For many Christians today, the threat of
separation from God, now and for eternity, is nonexistent. As
Irish poet Patrick Kavanaugh writes in one of his poems about
lost childhood religion, "the knife of penance fell so like a blade /
Of grass that no one was afraid."

Yet some of the most repeated prayers in history are pleadings
with God to spare loved ones from the torments of hell. One
medieval theologian advised, "Let us not cease by alms, and
intercessions, to appease Him who hath power to cast, but doth
not always use this power, but is able to pardon also." Medieval
prayer books even included the following prayer, to be used by
the faithful for a loved one whose earthly deeds were particularly
lacking in merit:

> O, Almighty and merciful God, incline, we beseech thee, thy
> holy ears unto our poorest prayers, which we do humbly
> pour forth before the sight of thy majesty, for the soul of
> thy servant _____, that forasmuch as we are distrustful
> of the quality of his life, by the abundance of thy pity we
> may be comforted; and if his soul cannot obtain full pardon,
> yet at least in the midst of the torments themselves, which
> peradventure it suffereth, out of the abundance of thy
> compassion it may feel refreshment.

Prayers such as these were removed from our prayer books long ago. Similarly, we pass easily over verses in the psalms such as "The friendship of the LORD is for those who fear him, and he makes his covenant known to them. My eyes are ever toward the LORD, for he will pluck my feet out of the net" (Psalm 25:14-15).

Faithfulness to the saints has clearly decreased over the centuries as our fear of hell and damnation has eased. Centuries ago, litanies of the saints were recited over a child just before baptism. A newborn would hear these great names before oil and chrism were added to the holy water and he or she was immersed in it three times. These saints were meant to be the infant's protectors. We seem to require less protection today.

The *Catechism of the Catholic Church*, however, in paragraphs 1030 to 1031, explains how purgatory is still a part of church doctrine:

> All who die in God's grace and friendship, but still imperfectly purified, are indeed assured of their eternal salvation; but after death they undergo purification, so as to achieve the holiness necessary to enter the joy of heaven.
>
> The Church gives the name purgatory to this final purification of the elect, which is entirely different from the punishment of the damned. The Church formulated her doctrine of faith on purgatory especially at the Councils of Florence [1439] and Trent [1563]. The tradition of the Church, by reference to certain texts of Scripture, speaks of a cleansing fire.

That is the only reference to purgatory in the current *Catechism*. According to church doctrine, the "cleansing fire" of purgatory is different from what is referred to as the "consuming fire" of hell. The difference between the two is simple: purgatory's sufferings are temporary and always have a blessed end. The real architect of purgatory, the poet Dante, wrote of the cleansing purpose of the place, "which rights in you what the world bent awry."[1]

Purgatory had been a solid feature of church tradition since the fourth century. As one translator of Dante explained: "All sins . . . are forgiven when the sinner repents in the name of

111

Christ, yet punishment may still be due; a kind but just father may forgive his son, yet for the son's own sake require some form of restitution, even when that restitution is as nothing in comparison with the gravity of the sin. A different way to look at it is that the sin is forgiven but the effects of the sin linger, and those effects have to be scoured away."[2] Despite purgatory's firm place in tradition, abuses of the doctrine became legion in the late Middle Ages.

Long gone are the sermons of preachers—the very preachers who so enraged Martin Luther that he wrote his biting attacks of them, and the church, turning the Christian world upside down—urging believers to give money to holy causes in exchange for their loved ones spending fewer days of purification in purgatory. It is not that long ago that devotions to the saints still resembled what Luther was protesting at the time of the Reformation. Luther railed against the sale of indulgences—church-granted remissions of the temporal and purgatorial punishment of sin—but he and others also questioned the promises made by the church to the faithful who practiced certain devotions. It was not long ago that the Holy See still published a popular devotional book entitled *The Raccolta of Prayers and Devotions Enriched with Indulgences,* known as *Preces et Pia Opera* in Latin. The word *raccolta* is Italian for "collection." The third enlarged edition of this classic book (published in 1938) includes this "devout practice" under the category "The Holy Trinity"; it is devotion #94:

> The faithful who, during the month of January,
> perform some special act of devotion
> in honor of the holy Name of Jesus are granted:
> An indulgence of 7 years once on any
> day of the month;
> A plenary indulgence under the usual
> conditions, if this act of devotion is
> repeated daily for the entire month.

And devotion #463, under the category "Angels and Saints," includes:

> The faithful who devoutly recite before an image of
> [Saint Stanislaus Kostka]:

"Our Father, Hail Mary," and "Glory be," adding the
invocation: "Saint Stanislaus, pray for me!" may obtain:
An indulgence of 300 days.

Each of these indulgences is applicable to a soul in purgatory.
Today, however, this sort of thing is almost as foreign to the
average Catholic as it is to those of us outside the tradition.
Protestants are reminded of number eighty-two of Luther's
Ninety-five Theses, in which he asks, "If the pope has the power
to grant an escape from Purgatory when a trivial fee is paid for an
indulgence, why doesn't he just empty Purgatory out of love for
the souls there?" Most of us think little of the goings-on of a purgatory for reasons along similar lines.

Indulgences also form part of the sacrament of penance in the
Catholic church today. These prescribed devotions and penances
are usually aimed at alleviating what is called the "temporal
punishment" of sin. God alone may forgive the eternal punishment of sin, but it is the church's responsibility to show people
how to purify themselves from the effects and attachments of sin.
As paragraph 1478 of the *Catechism* states: "An indulgence is
obtained through the Church who, by virtue of the power of
binding and loosing granted her by Jesus Christ, intervenes in favor
of individual Christians and opens for them the treasury of the
merits of Christ and the saints to obtain from the Father of
mercies the remission of the temporal punishments due for
their sins."

Martin Luther's radical reform made it possible for people
to believe as they wished. By diminishing the power of the
church so that it no longer exclusively held the keys to heaven
and hell, the Protestant Reformation created the first aspects of
consumer-driven religion.

WHAT LUTHER DID

The Protestant Reformation of the early sixteenth century—
the single greatest watershed in Christianity—was primarily a
triumph of ideas. It resulted in nothing short of a new definition
of what it meant to be Christian.

Before Luther's radical triumph, the church viewed itself as
the interpreter of God's revelation, and the primary tool for this

113

interpretation was tradition. Not only was tradition the primary criterion for determining truth, but it also was assumed that truth deliberately communicated itself through tradition.

Devotion to the saints was an uncontested feature of daily life all over Europe until about one century before Luther. In the churches, lamps would be left perpetually shining before images of the saints, and daily Masses were said at their altars. In England in the fifteenth century, the church decreed that certain days each year—at least fifty of them, not including Sundays—were to be dedicated to specific saints. On these days, just as on Sundays, no work was to be done and no business transacted. The faithful were required to fast on the evening before each of these festival days and then to be present at the daily services of Mass, morning prayer, and evening prayer.[3]

The situation changed dramatically over a short period of time when Protestant ideas caught fire. The triumph of Protestantism was devastating for popular devotion to the saints. When the Reformation took hold in towns throughout England and Europe, anything related to the saints was suspect and subject to removal—physical, spiritual, and ecclesiastical—from religious life.

John Wycliffe and the Lollards in England, the preacher Savaronola in Florence, and others had denounced abuses that had built up in the late-medieval church—such as corrupt priests and the sale of indulgences—and had often died for their stands. The time had not been right for the radical transfer of spiritual power that came with Luther's revolution. Luther was prompted to make his stand by Pope Leo X, who, in order to fund the construction of St. Peter's Basilica in Rome, had inseparably linked the purchasing of indulgences (assurances of reduced time in purgatory or even salvation written on small pieces of paper) with true piety. Devotion to a saint had become for many simply one more means of finding a bit of favor with God, easily purchased, and from Luther's time forward, true devotion was tainted. Later in life, Luther recalled how he felt at that time about the buying and selling of indulgences: "[It] was demolishing heaven and consuming the earth with fire."[4]

Other reformers, such as Paul Giustiniani—who later founded the order of Camaldolese Hermits (named for Camaldoli, Italy) to fix errors in and rejuvenate right monastic practice—attempted to reach Leo X in the years leading up to Luther's reforms, but to no avail. Paul Giustiniani's urgings, in 1513, included the need for vernacular translations of Scripture and other causes that foreshadowed the reforms of the first Protestants, but they did not cut to the root of religious power, as Luther's reforms soon did.

Luther was a young Augustinian monk, and his campaign against the abuses of religious power in regard to devotional practices and spirituality pitted him against a Dominican priest and theologian named Johann Tetzel ("A great ranter . . . selling grace for money as dearly or as cheaply as he could," Luther later wrote of him).[5] In many ways their dispute was an intrareligious one between two rival monastic movements, each vying for superiority in scholarship. Luther knew the Bible very well, and his arguments were sound, and in the end it was his ideas that triumphed over the tradition which Tetzel espoused. Luther won the hearts and minds of many ordinary laypeople, and of many more powerful princes and governors also anxious to wrest some control from Rome. His Ninety-five Theses, published against Tetzel, the pope, and the practice of indulgences, "went throughout the whole of Germany in a fortnight," wrote Luther later in life, "for the whole world complained about [them]."[6]

Before Luther, the traditions of the church were usually accepted without question as the primary means of God's revelation to humanity. When Luther and others began to seriously challenge the origins and validity of tradition and to turn attention back to the New Testament Scriptures and the picture that emerges there of the practices used in the first decades after Christ's ministry, they were challenging the most fundamental ideas of Christianity. They were redefining what it meant to be Christian. Luther was suggesting that all the theologians in the world, all the popes in history, and all the accumulated tradition that the church represented meant nothing if they did not conform to the desires of God and the ministry that Christ began. In his tract "On Christian Liberty," published in 1520, Luther wrote:

> To cast everything aside, even speculation, meditations, and
> whatever things can be performed by the exertions of the
> soul itself, is of no profit. One thing, and one alone, is

necessary for life, justification, and Christian liberty; and that is the most holy word of God, the Gospel of Christ.

There are many differences between spiritual practice in medieval religion and religion of today. Especially for Protestants—but also for many Catholics since the Second Vatican Council—the primary change is that today we usually feel free to *choose* when and how to practice. Luther wouldn't have liked this sort of individualism at all, but it is the effect of his challenging the church of his day and redefining the faith.

THE BABY AND THE BATHWATER

"For faith alone," Luther continued in *On Christian Liberty,* "and the efficacious use of the word of God, bring salvation. . . . The word of God cannot be received and honored by any works, but by faith alone." His reliance on faith alone, as a corrective measure against medieval religion, led Luther to despise most traditional expressions of the spiritual life. He considered most devotions and pieties, outside the basic duties of moral obedience, to be works that reeked of meaningless effort expended in order to merit heaven. Luther taught that the things the faithful did to know, obey, and experience a life in Christ were not necessities. Righteousness is given freely by the God who justifies by faith alone, according to Luther. Works are something else.

Therefore, with these swift denunciations, Luther and the first Protestants tossed out the baby (tradition, devotions, pieties) with the bathwater (the belief that tradition, devotions, and pieties would justify one before God). Luther's teaching that spiritual works or practices would not earn a person heaven led directly to the doing away with most works and practices. Faith became belief centered rather than practice centered, and belief and practice remain separate in many of our lives even today.

Taking cues from the apostle Paul's letter to the Romans, Luther claimed that the primary responsibility of any Christian was to accept God's grace of salvation by faith alone. Like St. Augustine before him, Luther had tried to find God in many ways—he had tried to attain by strenuous effort what he later believed was attainable only by God's grace—but now he quickly came to believe that to expend great effort in penance, piety, and obedience to every rule and suggestion from the church and tradition was foolishness. The ones doing the fooling and the controlling of the salvation of others, in Luther's mind, were the leaders of the Roman Catholic church.

Luther and other Protestant theologians believed that venerations of the saints and images of them were the product of idolatry. John Calvin, Luther's contemporary in Geneva, taught that "the human mind is a perpetual forge of idols." In other words, Christians must continuously fight the tendency to make heroes into idols. Preaching was seen as the ideal antidote to this and other forms of idolatry. The early Reformers felt their task was to educate the simpleminded who venerated saints rather than God alone.

For Luther, salvation was simple: One could do nothing to gain it, salvation could only be accepted as a free gift. He was able to preach this with confidence because he also believed that the Scriptures alone testified God's truth to believers. In other words, an interpreter, or a priest, a bishop, or a pope, was unnecessary, and so was tradition—and so was, ultimately, the church. James Carroll, one of the most important Catholic historians writing today, offers the following summary of this aspect of Luther's reform and explains the Catholic response to it:

> One reason to be grateful to the Church of the Counter-Reformation is its resounding rejection . . . of Luther's primal idea that the Christian is to be guided by *sola scriptura,* Scripture alone. In reaction to the abuses of Church authority that drove Luther to his radical stance, he appealed to the ultimate authority of the Bible, as if the texts preceded the community that reads them. But the Catholic position was, and remains, that the community, albeit an inspired community, produced those texts as inspired texts, and they are nothing without the readers who take them in. . . . Luther rejected what appeared to him to be the Church's idolatry of its own hierarchy, but despite his best intentions, he replaced it with a deference to the Word that slips all too easily into an idolatry of its own.[7]

Other doctrines that Luther introduced overturned the traditions of the church as well. "Justification by faith alone" meant that ultimately the system of sacraments and the institution of the church that administered and supported them were unnecessary for salvation. "The priesthood of all believers" meant that each person could have a direct relationship with God, unmediated by clergy or tradition. The cumulative effect of these teachings—published in tract form and spread all over Europe with the help of a new invention, the printing press— was a revolutionary transfer of spiritual power from the church to the individual believer.

The individual is of utmost importance in much of Protestant practice and in the body of believers; religious authority and tradition is a clear second. The radical nature of these ideas was then compounded when Luther placed new emphasis on the Christian doctrine of original sin, which is the notion that the first human sin of Adam and Eve in the Garden has been passed on to every succeeding generation; the original sin of our first parents taints us from the moment we emerge from the womb. Luther said that popes and cardinals and theologians were no different from the rest of us before God. We all begin with this same ultimate handicap, and we all achieve salvation, or reconciliation with God, through faith alone. It is not difficult to see why many historians point to Luther as one of the forerunners of modern democracy.

This single idea—for it really does boil down to one single idea—has transformed religion and spiritual understanding ever since. Even freethinking Catholics today—those who opt to follow their conscience rather than church teaching on certain moral questions—are children of Luther. For most of us today, truth is communicated individually, not through tradition.

Notice how much we have been taught to rely on this single, radical idea. Reflect also on the logic of it and how our Protestant conclusions, so marvelous in many ways and full of opportunity, nevertheless create an ideological environment that spurns many of the ways that centuries of Christians before us used to deepen their friendship with and understanding of God. It is no wonder that our spiritual lives are so often stuck in our heads and that so many of us are delighting in learning spiritual practices for the first time—as if they are new to Christianity itself.

Tradition does not play much of a role in many Protestants' lives, while for many Catholics the idea of converting to Protestantism over disagreements with church teaching is out of the question. James Joyce's autobiographical character, Stephen Dedalus, expresses this humorously in a conversation with a friend about fading faith in tradition versus the Protestant notion of following the individual conscience:

> —Then, said Cranly, you do not intend to become a protestant?
> —I said that I had lost the faith, Stephen answered, but not that I had lost self-respect. What kind of liberation would that be to forsake an absurdity which is logical and coherent and to embrace one which is illogical and incoherent?[8]

Ultimately, we might want to ask ourselves: Does God reside first and foremost in our individual souls and minds, or first in the community of the faithful? Protestants have rejected popes, bishops, and priests and have mocked with disdain, or squirmed with discomfort around, those who suggest that traditions or religious authorities are necessary mediators between God and the human soul. Many Protestants regard the making of saints in the same way. We believe, on the one hand, that they are unnecessary when direct communication with God is easy and possible and, on the other hand, that all Christians are equally justified before God, making it inappropriate to position certain individuals somehow above the rest.

Luther's great contributions were colloquial translations of the Scriptures, made available to all laypeople; catechisms that explained doctrine in simple terms; hymnbooks that allowed people to worship in their own language; and expository preaching. All these things aimed to teach the Bible and do away with the penitential system of earning salvation. Luther "called for the reduction of Church festivals and a curb on pilgrimages. Saints should be left to canonize themselves."[9] He did not directly overturn the practices related to the communion of the saints, but when he came to that portion of the Apostles' Creed in his *Small Catechism*, he redefined the communion of saints as "the whole Church on earth . . . with Jesus in the one, true faith."

OTHER EARLY PROTESTANTS AND ANTI-CATHOLICISM

Other Protestants took Luther's denouncing of the Catholic church a few steps further. John Foxe (1516–87), who was a product of the Catholic-on-Protestant and Protestant-on-Catholic violence of sixteenth-century England, added to his *Book of Martyrs* the subtitle *A History of the Lives, Sufferings and Triumphant Deaths of the Early Christian and the Protestant Martyrs*. Foxe spoke for Puritans then and many Protestants now when he linked the martyrs of the early church—with their passion, faith, and commitment to the gospel and Christ—with the Protestant martyrs of Catholic violence in the sixteenth century. He began chapter 4, "Papal Persecutions," with this paragraph:

> Thus far our history of persecution has been confined principally to the pagan world. We come now to a period when persecution, under the guise of Christianity, committed more enormities than ever disgraced the annals of paganism. Disregarding the maxims and the spirit of the Gospel, the papal Church, arming herself with the power of the sword, vexed the Church of God and wasted it for several centuries, a period most appropriately termed in history, the "dark ages." The kings of the earth, gave their power to the "Beast," and submitted to be trodden on by the miserable vermin that often filled the papal chair, as in the case of Henry, emperor of Germany. The storm of papal persecution first burst upon the Waldensians in France.

And Foxe's next paragraph highlights what is still today the dominant Protestant attitude toward the effect of the Roman Catholic church on the Christian faith:

> Popery having brought various innovations into the Church, and overspread the Christian world with darkness and superstition, some few, who plainly perceived the pernicious tendency of such errors, determined to show the light of the Gospel in its real purity, and to disperse those clouds which artful priests had raised about it, in order to blind the people, and obscure its real brightness.

Other early Puritans sought to reform religion in England by removing all "popery" or "Romish" elements, as they popularly referred to Catholic piety in order to demonstrate its bastardizing effect on what was seen as true, apostolic faith. In one "Admonition to Parliament" in 1572, Puritan leaders denounced the Anglican Book of Common Prayer as "an imperfect book, culled and picked out of the popish dunghill." They sought a more radical separation from the traditions of medieval faith. Puritans, like some Protestants today, endeavored to do away with all elements of Catholic sacraments and worship that they believed departed from the apostolic church: making the sign of the cross, rings offered in marriage, the calendar of saints, candles and incense, missals and prayer manuals, clergy vestments and liturgical colors and symbolism of all kinds, organ music, and bowing and kneeling, just to name several.[10]

Other contemporaries of Luther also acknowledged what was wrong with the church and sought to eradicate the abuses but nevertheless remained Catholic. Erasmus was one such person. He is called the "prince of the humanists" because of his dedication to the ideals of the Renaissance. He was educated all over Europe and had close relationships with the kings of England, France, and Spain, as well as Pope Leo X, who admired Erasmus's learning and shielded him from the zealots of the church who accused the popular teacher of secretly aligning himself with the Protestant Reformers.

The most famous intellectual of his day, trusted by popes and kings, Erasmus was able to write and teach in ways that would probably have been condemned if they had been done by someone else. In his humorous *Colloquies,* Erasmus poked fun at the many foolish and superstitious ways that people were devoted to saints. He was critical of people's motivations on pilgrimages, during confessions, and in prayerful intercessions to the saints. For example, in this passage Erasmus imagines the Virgin Mary commiserating in a letter with one of Luther's students:

> We take in good part your strenuous endeavors [as a true disciple of Luther] to convince the world of the vanity and needlessness of invoking saints. For I was even wearied out of my life with importunities, petitions, and complaints.

121

Everybody comes to me as if my son were to be always a child, because he is painted so. And because they see him still at my breast they take for granted that he dares deny me nothing that I ask him for fear that, when he has a mind to it, I should deny him the bubby.

Erasmus has Mary continue her complaint, caricaturing the different requests that people make of the saints, emphasizing the futility and superstition of it all:

Their requests are sometimes so extravagant that I am ashamed to mention them.

The merchant when he is to make a long voyage, desires me to take care of his concubine. The professed nun, when she is to make her escape, recommends to me the care of her reputation. The gambler prays to me for a good hand at dice, and promises me a portion of his profits.

The maidens pray for rich and handsome husbands. The wives for fair children. The big-bellied for easy labor. The philosopher prays for the faculty to start difficulties that can never be resolved.

In Erasmus's farce, Mary concludes: "If I deny them anything, I am considered hard-hearted. If I send them to my son, their answer is, if you'll say the word I'm sure he'll do it."

Most interestingly, Mary then adds a warning to this imaginary follower of Luther, who may wish to do as Luther's most enthusiastic followers were beginning to do all over Europe by tearing down statues and art devoted to the saints: removing them by force from the lives of people who love them. Mary says:

This trouble is almost over now, for which I am thankful, but only if you would stop here, which they say you will not, until you have stripped the altars as well as the saints. Let me advise you, over and over, to take care in what you do, for you will find that the saints are prepared better for revenge than you may realize. What will you get by throwing Peter out of the Church, when he comes to keep you out of heaven? Paul has a sword; Bartholomew has a knife. What will you do when you encounter George on horseback with his spear? And Anthony himself has his holy fire. None of the saints are unable, one way or another, to do you mischief if he pleases.

This is how the great intellectual avoided the wrath of the church authorities of his day, despite his frequent critiques of the abuses all around them. Even though motivations were called into question, and the reasons for appealing to the saints were widely criticized as irrelevant and just plain wrong, most people besides the new Protestants were not ready to throw aside the saints, their stories, and the ways in which they still live among us.

My own branch of the Protestant tradition traces its roots back to the early church and the subsequent founding of the Church of England. Despite its heritage, the Anglican tradition, in its original document, the Thirty-nine Articles (which approximates to a creed and was adopted in 1563), was once dismissive of the veneration of saints with a bigotry common in Protestant documents of the time:

> The Romish Doctrine concerning Purgatory, Pardons, Worshipping, and Adoration as well of Images of Relics, and also invocation of saints, is a fond thing vainly invented, and grounded upon no warranty of Scripture, but rather repugnant to the Word of God. (Article 22)

Most Episcopalians in America, and Anglicans elsewhere, would be surprised to learn that their church had once said such a thing as this. But the Thirty-nine Articles, in its tone and fervent anti-Rome sentiment, was influenced by the Protestant movement that was sweeping Europe.

It has been a slow recovery for Protestants trying to overcome the fiery words of the sixteenth-century Protestant Reformation.

Luther's theological argument and Erasmus's satire represent two of the ways that devotions to the saints were debunked five hundred years ago. Fear and prejudice have also played a part. Two hundred years after Luther, the Enlightenment-era historian Edward Gibbon extended the Protestant critique of Catholic piety, blaming it for the very fall of the Roman Empire. In his classic *History of the Decline and Fall of the Roman Empire* (1776–88), Gibbon wrote of those "hideous, distorted, and emaciated maniacs, without knowledge, without patriotism, without affection, spending their lives in a long routine of useless and atrocious tortures and quailing before the ghastly phantoms of their delirious brains." Gibbon was criticizing monks, and his criticism of them, as well as his interpretations of Western religious history, has had long-standing and deep influence, even on the way that many of us view the role of spiritual people in society today. Gibbon taught us that by separating themselves—spiritually or physically—from the dominant culture, those who become saints first demonstrate traits that are not very admirable: cowardice, weakness, a lack of patriotism, selfishness, and carelessness for the needs of others.

Gibbon's ideas are still very much with us. Throughout the world, the critique of Catholic piety continues. England versus Ireland, the United States versus Mexico—they may sound like World Cup matches, but they also represent clashes of worldviews, the first in each pair priding itself on rationalism and the second priding itself on mystery and tradition.

One century after the Enlightenment, Friedrich Nietzsche, the son of a Lutheran minister, made known his detestation of saints and devotions, sounding much like Gibbon. One of Nietzsche's bugaboos was what he called "the will to power," which characterizes and afflicts us; this is our striving to dominate one another. Nietzsche suggested that saints and martyrs actually attempted to dominate the rest of us with their asceticism. The German philosopher saw an insidious, even odious, "will to power" in the tears, fasting, and self-immolation of the saintly. He called it a "striving for distinction" of an awful sort.

In their very discreetness and indirectness (which is, of course, part and parcel of godliness in the tradition of Jesus), Christian techniques of sainthood were, for Nietzsche, nothing less than domination. Nietzsche took the paranoid playground accusation "Do you think you are better than me?" to new levels. He was afraid that anyone who tried to be righteous was in possession of ulterior motives. Such a person "is quite satisfied with the impression he makes on us: he wants to conceal from us his [true] desire [for the world], his pride, his intention to soar beyond us."[11]

Like Dante, who placed his greatest enemies in the lowest circles of hell, Nietzsche reserved for saints and martyrs his lowest depth: that of striving to distinguish oneself from one's contemporaries. The ascetic, martyr, or saint, according to Nietzsche, does not impose direct torment and hardship on others—as do less-sophisticated men and women practicing the "will to power"—but, instead, they destroy the happiness of others by imposing torment and hardship on themselves. What brilliance! Nietzsche seems to say. What conniving! Happiness, the philosopher seems to believe, goes hand in hand with power, and for this reason the saint finds the most satisfaction.

Nietzsche referred to this saintly striving for distinction over others as an example of the "extravagance of the lust for power." He believed that saints not only reveled in their self-imposed torments (which they sometimes did: see part three of this book), but that they also created and sustained a world (and an underworld) where all people must either suffer now or suffer later. In these ways, saintly power was "voluptuous," he said.

Nietzsche's ideas have also had their effect on the popular perception of saints. Kathryn Harrison, author of a recent biography of Thérèse of Lisieux, paints an engaging and sympathetic portrait of the saint but also throws in the occasional Nietzschean zinger. About Thérèse's more dramatic spiritual experiences, Harrison writes: "Ecstasies are unforgettable, and they are tyrannical. Those who experience them helplessly shape their lives in order to create the possibility of another encounter with the holy."[12] The person who lives today in ways that are deliberately aimed at sainthood is perceived to be an idealist, probably deluded, and a threat to those around him or her who know better.

THE LAST WORD OF PROTESTANTISM?

Paul Tillich, a prominent theologian from the last century, offered what he called "the Protestant principle," which simply states: "The first word of religion must be spoken against religion." This self-correction is the essence of what I would call the overriding Protestant impulse to disbelieve. We will best know what is true if we are never settled with truth. Doubt is the first and last word of what it means to be Protestant.

But why is disbelief such a virtue when the passion of its opposite can yield such amazing results? I believe that people who do great things act with little doubt. Mahatma Gandhi wrote in his autobiography: "I am far from claiming any finality or infallibility about my conclusions. One claim I do indeed make and it is this. For me they appear to be absolutely correct, and seem for the time being to be final. For if they were not, I should base no action on them." Isn't that the very perspective of a great saint? Protestant doubt stands in the way of the sort of clarity of mind and purpose that creates great saints.

We Protestants need to ask ourselves: Why is it that Catholics seem to do a better job of creating saints than we do? Could the Presbyterian church in America have created an Oscar Romero? Have Protestant missionaries to India created a Mother Teresa? Could my own Episcopal church have nurtured a Dorothy Day? Could Protestant faith have formed a Seraphim of Sarov, the holy fool of Russia? Probably not, but why? As a lifelong Protestant and also a lover of the early and medieval church—before the reforms of Martin Luther and others in the sixteenth century—I am convinced that we must try to discover what makes a saint and why it seems to be such an exclusively Catholic and Orthodox thing. Bear in mind, I don't mean to ask: Why do Catholics believe in the presence of saints? But rather: Why do Catholics seem to be able to *produce* them?

Practices

Mitch Finley

M ITCH FINLEY IS AN AWARD-WINNING CATHOLIC author of many popular books, including *The Joy of Being Catholic*, *Prayer for People Who Think Too Much*, and *The Seeker's Guide to Saints*.

First, I want to make it clear that, as with any Catholic whose faith is balanced, any relationships I have with saints are secondary to my relationship with the risen Christ and in the context of the church understood as the communion of saints—a communion, or community, that exists in both time and eternity. Thus, all devotion to and veneration of saints is "in Christ." A balanced Catholic spirituality never acts as if saints have some power independent of the power of God. The point of the communion of saints, here, is the belief that those who have died may pray for us in eternity, just as we pray for one another in time and space.

127

Given all this, the saint who is most important to me is Mary, the mother of Jesus. But on occasion I also relate to saints such as St. Thérèse of Lisieux, St. Anthony of Padua, and St. Joseph. These are all canonized saints to whom the Catholic church approves a public devotion. At the same time, on a private level I also relate to some uncanonized "saints"—e.g., Thomas Merton, Dorothy Day—and ask for their prayers. For that matter, also on a private level I sometimes communicate with other members of the communion of saints, such as deceased loved ones— e.g., my mother and grandmother.

I have had a devotion to the Blessed Virgin Mary since childhood. Catholics believe that Mary has a unique relationship with her son; plus, I admire the way she is portrayed in various New Testament documents. I was introduced to devotion to Mary early in life. The nuns who taught in the Catholic schools I attended were, no doubt, quite instrumental in this. One of the first learning experiences I can remember in a Catholic school was hearing a nun explain the difference between the adoration of God and the veneration of the Blessed Virgin Mary and other saints.

I carry a rosary in my pocket at most times, and I pray the rosary fairly often. Sometimes when I, or someone I know, have lost something, I ask St. Anthony to pray for the lost object's return—a traditional form of Catholic devotion. In especially desperate situations, usually in the lives of others, I say a prayer to St. Jude, the patron saint of hopeless causes, asking for his prayers.

8

Wonder-Working and the
Difficulty of Belief

SCOTT HAHN IS THE MOST POPULAR CATHOLIC AUTHOR in America today, aside from Pope John Paul II himself. With the fervor for tradition so often found in a convert (Hahn converted from evangelical Protestantism to Catholicism in 1986), he tackles in his books the topics that separate Catholics and Protestants most clearly: the Mass *(The Lamb's Supper: The Mass as Heaven on Earth)*; the Virgin Mary *(Hail, Holy Queen: The Mother of God in the Word of God)*; the sacrament of confession *(Lord, Have Mercy: The Healing Power of Confession)*; and the power of the sacraments—seven rather than the Protestant two, or none—in everyday life *(Swear to God: The Promise and Power of the Sacraments)*. I expect that Hahn might eventually write about purgatory, papal infallibility, and the miracles of the saints, which would nearly complete the cycle of issues that most divide us today.

Hahn's books are popular because in addition to being concise and well-written, they remind Catholics today of what their parents and grandparents taught them to believe. They are filled with traditional ideas and new ways of looking at and accepting them. His books are perfectly attuned to the teachings that have come from the Vatican in the past twenty-five years under John Paul II, a very traditional and conservative thinker, as they remind people of "the way things used to be."

I suspect that Hahn sometimes intends, in his explanations of what Catholics believe, to leave not only most Protestants, but also many progressive Catholics, cold. For example, in his book on the sacrament of confession (which is not considered a sacrament in any Protestant churches), he writes under the heading "Who Needs a Priest?":

> Non-Catholics often object that the priest is unnecessary in this process, that Christians can confess their sins directly to God. No doubt we can; but we cannot be assured of forgiveness unless we go about our confession in the way that God Himself intended.[1]

Hahn likewise defends the church's doctrine of the "perpetual virginity" of Mary, which states that Mary and Joseph never consummated their marriage. Dismissively rehearsing the most common objections that Protestants have had to this teaching, with frequent allusion to ancient debates that took place between St. Jerome and others, he concludes:

> It is clear from Scripture and Tradition that she lived her virginity—so much that, for all future generations, she became its very personification.[2]

There is not much here to satisfy those of us who follow the "Protestant principle."

John Henry Newman was another Protestant who converted to Catholicism. In the middle of the nineteenth century, Newman anticipated many objections to Catholic teachings by criticizing the excessive Protestant reliance on satisfying doubt. Newman believed that he himself was guilty of a rationalistic tendency. According to Newman, too much rationality was equivalent to "false liberty of thought, or the exercise of thought upon matters in which, from the constitution of the human mind, thought cannot be brought to any successful issue." Newman's solution to the problem was to turn to what he called "revealed truth," or faithful reliance on the truth of the church and tradition, just as Scott Hahn does today.

This sort of reasoning will not satisfy many of our critical, modern minds (and I realize that Newman would say, "It is not supposed to!"). There is a large distance between Protestant over-rationality and doubt and Catholic overreliance on tradition as the arbiter of truth. Nowhere is this conflict seen more clearly than in our attitudes toward the miraculous.

MIRACLES IN THE LIVES OF THE SAINTS

Instances of wonder-working punctuate the lives of saints at every turn, and millions of people around the world today believe in these works without hesitation. To a mind and an imagination schooled to believe, rather than not believe, the miraculous is very close to the natural order of events. Although many of the miraculous stories in the lives of the saints read more like fairy tales than history, it is also true that reliable miracles have happened, and even before skeptics' very eyes.

Not all saints have been mystics and wonder-workers. Bernard of Clairvaux was a great teacher but was most influential as an organizer, politician, and motivator. He lived at the center of European politics during the era of the Crusades, influencing not only popes but emperors and princes as well. Similarly, Vincent de Paul (d. 1660) led a life of remarkable efficiency: he was a minister to the prisoners of pre-Revolution Paris, a trainer of priests who cared for peasants in the French countryside, and the administrator of eleven seminaries. We should remember his life and his example even though he was not led to do what he did by visions, angels, or mystical experiences. Augustine of Hippo, also, was no mystic but was perhaps the most important theologian and writer in the history of the faith. Neither the touch of his hands nor the desires of his mind resulted in miracles. Catherine of Siena, on the other hand, combined a mystical life with a political one. She was a counsel to popes and integral in arranging for the pope's return to Rome from exile in Avignon, France. Many of the saints lived ordinary lives without mystical experiences; many others lived mystical lives that still seem within reach of ordinary people.

Some writers, anxious to depict the romantic spirit of the Middle Ages, exaggerate the role of miracles in the lives of saints. For instance, art historian Emile Mâle writes: "A true saint was a man who saw angels and demons face to face. The story that the devil extinguished her candle at one side while an angel relighted it at the other, was the one episode in the legend of St. Genevieve which the people of Paris remembered."[3]

It is true, however, that, particularly before the modern era, nothing grabbed the attention of the faithful as did stories of miraculous events. These happenings signaled that God was not far away and was available to those who called on him. Those who heard of miracles easily believed them. The first explanation for the unexpected—life or death, meteorological events, objects found that had long been forgotten, good or bad "luck"—was divine intervention. Some miracle stories even made good sense, but stories of wonder-working also became a kind of literary form for the telling of tales involving holy men and women. Certain expectations arose that justified the inclusion of fantastic stories in the lives of the saints, especially if they were stories similar to those found in earlier lives of the saints and as long as they were attested to by one reliable witness.

The most important historian of early Britain, Venerable Bede, for instance, fills his histories with miraculous accounts under these pretenses. A formula was easily applied to subsequent lives of the saints, and it is easy to note, after reading a number of these stories, that many of the saints seem to have practiced the same miracles. We frequently read of healings of the needy; physical struggles with the devil or demons; heroic salvations from the clutches of beasts; allusions to biblical miracles—particularly those of Moses or Jesus—sleep deprivation as a result of intimacy with and meditation on God; and extraordinary fasting, particularly subsistence on the Eucharist alone.

Miraculous stories of fasting, in fact, are intended to symbolize the complete sustenance that can be found only in God. One late-twentieth-century soon-to-be saint, Marthe Robin of France, "lived," according to the Vatican, "for 53 years consuming nothing more than the Holy Eucharist." Many other people have gone for periods of time doing the same. People such as Padre Pio and Marthe Robin, Catholic legend says, are able to do these remarkable things because they are "chosen souls who live such a degree of union with Christ that the physical body is taken into and affected by such union."[4] This natural blending of the miraculous and everyday life, unquestioned by the devout, is why lives of the saints are usually referred to as hagiography.

Some of the greatest minds of the premodern era believed in the wonder-working powers of holy women and men. While these stories are extremely difficult for us to take seriously today, they edified their original hearers and readers. "They learned from them that God was still ruling in spite of the many troubles that harassed the lives of ordinary men, and that from time to time He could still intervene on their behalf."[5]

Gerald of Wales, considered one of the best historians of his day, wrote the following account of an ordinary daily miracle around the year 1200:

> It happened . . . that a boy tried to steal some young pigeons from a nest in Saint David's church in Llanfaes [Wales]. His hand stuck fast to the stone on which he was leaning, this being no doubt a miraculous punishment inflicted by the Saint, who was protecting the birds of his own church. For three days and nights the boy, accompanied by his parents and his friends, offered vigils, fasts and prayers at the church altar. On the third day, by God's intervention, the power which held his hand fast was loosened and he was released from the miraculous force which bound him there to the stone. I myself saw this same boy, then no longer young but become an old man living in Newbury in England, for so the years had passed, when he appeared before David II, Bishop of St David's, and confirmed that these events really had occurred.[6]

Blaise Pascal, the great seventeenth-century physicist and mathematician, believed in the power of religious relics to perform miracles. His niece was once cured of an eye ailment after a thorn of Jesus' crown of thorns was touched to it. In *Pensées* (#854), Pascal explains that God chooses the places, subjects, and vehicles of miraculous action, and that, in this case, "God chose this house in which to blaze his power."

At other times, miracles seem entirely reasonable, and even some of those in the pages of medieval hagiographies express something both miraculous and attainable in the world today.

> By divine grace I have several times experienced a miraculous enlarging of the grasp of the mind so that I seemed to look at the whole world caught in one ray of sunlight.[7]

Some skeptics throughout history have tried to authenticate miracle claims from the lives of the saints. Tim Severin is one of the most interesting of these in recent years. In 1975–76, he determined to show himself and the world what he thought could be true—that St. Brendan might have really sailed in a leather boat from the coast of Ireland to the New World in the Middle Ages. For Severin, and some scholars of medieval texts, the fantastic and unbelievable images from the ancient "Voyage of Brendan" were explainable.

> Seen in another light, the episodes in Brendan's voyage bore a striking resemblance to geographical facts. The floating pillar of crystal could have been an iceberg which the travelers had met at sea. Perhaps the sea monster was a pugnacious whale or a walrus. The burning rocks hurled at them might have been molten slag thrown up by an eruption in Iceland or in the Azores, which are both seats of volcanic activity.[8]

In fact, Severin and his crew of three successfully sailed a replica of the vessel (known as a curragh) depicted in the chronicle of Brendan's voyage across the North Atlantic, landing 300 miles north of St. John's, the Newfoundland capital. They covered the squarish hull of the thirty-six-foot curragh with treated ox hides, according to specifications provided by experts on medieval shipbuilding, Irish monasticism, and the treatment of leather before exposure to seawater.

The novelist Umberto Eco, who wrote the classic medieval-murder thriller, *The Name of the Rose*, once explained why we so often enjoy such simple stories as those of the exploits of James Bond, secret agent 007: "The reader's pleasure consists in finding himself plunged into a game where he knows the pieces and the rules and even (aside from some very minor variations) the outcome."[9] This is how we might approach the lives of the saints—as an opportunity to focus in on the unique and often extraordinary features of their personalities and commitments. The plots, it is true, run in remarkably similar directions and trajectories, but each saint's story has features that point to what is profoundly important for our own lives.

DEVELOPING THE CAPACITY
TO BELIEVE

In addition to reading the lives of the saints with the understanding that not all miracles should be taken literally, we also should probably learn to believe at different levels. This can be very difficult, particularly for those of us schooled in doubt and disbelief, but there is a difference between being credulous—believing easily and without reason—and developing a capacity to believe what is possible with God.

You may already be disappointed by the relative lack of miracles recounted in these pages. My Protestant imagination tells me that saints are important because of their deeds but not primarily because of their wonder-working. The stories of saints that are filled with their wondrous workings in the world do not often communicate the spirit of God as well as those that tell of saints who perform human acts of righteousness. St. Anthony of Padua (d. 1231) and St. Colette (d. 1447), for instance, are credited with reforming, respectively, the men's and women's orders created by Sts. Francis and Clare of Assisi. Yet the miracles of Anthony and Colette pile up in ways that are completely unbelievable; their lives are no match for the simple holiness of their spiritual father and mother. The lives of Francis and Clare are almost devoid of the unexplainable, and when miracles do seem to happen to them, or around them, they strive to hide the holiness. Francis and Clare each influenced others primarily through natural, human means—a teaching, a look, a glance, a touch, a gesture of mediation—rather than as magicians walking about the Umbrian countryside turning the natural world upside down.

There will never be a lack of miraculous stories of saints' doings in the world, and as we have seen, a few of them are necessary in order for saints to be beatified and canonized by the Vatican. However, miracle stories that are taken as the primary evidence of sainthood appeal chiefly to two categories of saint watchers: what I would term the actively devout and the rational defenders. The actively devout are involved with saints every day. They "live" with them at home, at work, and at play through prayer. Some of the spiritual practices of the actively devout are sprinkled throughout this book. Usually, they grew up with the saints in their lives, and they believe in miracles as easily as they believe in a parent's love.

I envy this sort of faith, where belief in miracles is easy and natural and, at the same time, completely unnecessary. In other words, miracles do not teach these faithful to believe, but rather belief teaches them that miracles are possible. They remind me of the followers (the "sheep") Jesus praises in this passage from the Gospel of John: "Jesus answered, 'I have told you, and you do not believe. The works that I do in my Father's name testify to me; but you do not believe, because you do not belong to my sheep. My sheep hear my voice. I know them, and they follow me" (John 10:25–27).

The rational defenders, on the other hand, appreciate the saints because they are an important part of tradition. These faithful know that prayer to the saints is efficacious and useful because tradition teaches that it is so. For the rational defenders, who are often converts to the faith, miracles attest to what can-not be known without faith: God intercedes in human affairs in ways that not only surprise us but also bypass or overrule science and common sense. In an ironic twist, rational faith (the seeking and debating of evidence that supports miracle claims) in some-thing inherently irrational (miracles) becomes a litmus test of faith for rational defenders. These believers remind me of a passage from the Gospel of John (quoted by Pascal as a reason *not* to believe in miracles): "Although he had performed so many signs in their presence, they did not believe in him. This was to fulfill the word spoken by the prophet Isaiah: 'Lord, who has believed our message, and to whom has the arm of the Lord been revealed?' And so they could not believe, because Isaiah also said, 'He has blinded their eyes and hardened their heart, so that they might not look with their eyes, and understand with their heart and turn—and I would heal them.' Isaiah said this because he saw his glory and spoke about him" (John 12:37–41).

The Bollandists, a school of the Jesuit order, were the most thorough rational defenders in the history of the Catholic church. In the eighteenth century, they undertook to demonstrate the undeniable truth of the lives of the saints, submitting legends to rigorous tests. The Bollandists' work was intended to counter the dismissive Protestant Reformers and the loss of faith brought on by the secular rationality of the early Enlightenment. Nevertheless, their tests for truth would not satisfy skeptics today.

One signal that the church evolves from era to era is that the methods of the Bollandists led to many of their members being charged with heresy at the time of the infamous Spanish Inquisition—because they lacked faith and doubted tradition— but more recently, the same methods have been officially endorsed by the Vatican. Jesuits make up the majority of today's Congregation for the Causes of Saints.

Do rational arguments really help clarify miracles for those who do not believe? Padre Pio, perhaps the most popular of the saints beatified or canonized in the past twenty years (more popular with Catholics, even, than Mother Teresa), was born in 1887 in the village of Pietrelcina in southern Italy. Brother Pio was baptized Francesco ("Francis") at an early age. Called Franci by family and friends, he entered the Franciscan order of Capuchins. As a new brother in the religious life, Pio underwent a stigmatization, and he also experienced several occasions of what is known as bilocation; that is, Padre Pio had the ability to respond to spiritual needs in two places at once by being physically present in both. He was not the first saint claimed to have experienced this phenomenon: St. Gerard Majella (d. 1755) reputedly did the same. Theologians, Vatican lawyers, and many other intelligent people, including millions of Roman Catholics around the world, believe these facts with as much certainty as they believe most anything else.

But it wasn't always so. Padre Pio was forced to undergo strenuous authentication of his stigmata wounds for fifty years. Although doctors authenticated them early on, Pope Pius XI had many doubts and responded by restricting Padre Pio's movement and contact with others. Both the Vatican and Padre Pio's superiors were loath to allow a simple country priest, or his brothers, to make grand spiritual claims—claims that would draw immense crowds of pilgrims seeking a blessing, a prayer, or a touch.

In the 1960s, the young bishop of Krakow, Karol Wojtyla, visited Padre Pio in Italy and then wrote a letter to the priest that has since become famous throughout the world. In the letter, Wojtyla asked for Padre Pio's prayers for a mother in Poland who had many children and was dying of cancer. Not only did the friar respond to the bishop that the woman would be healed, but he also declared that the bishop would one day become the bishop of Rome, the supreme pontiff of the church. Of course, Karol Wojtyla was indeed elected Pope John Paul II in 1978.

It is difficult for many Protestants to believe in these things today. We are not prepared for this sort of belief. We did not grow up hearing stories of saints and their miracles read at the dinner table, as did centuries of Catholic children. Most of us are not prepared to believe in quarks because we have not already been taught to believe in alpha decay, wave-particle duality, and blackbody radiation. In the same way, having not been exposed to belief in miracles, as out forefathers and fore-mothers were, we are not prepared to believe in them. Our planet was once the center of the universe, and the sun revolved around the earth—or so we believed, with evidence at our disposal. What we don't know for certain should never fail to astound us.

The Latin word for miracle (*miraculum*) literally means "something wonderful." Perhaps we give God less credit than God deserves. Miracles have fallen out of intellectual favor on the tails of other teachings now easily dismissed, such as God's providence, or the supernatural plans and designs for what happens in our lives. Today, we more often imagine a God with less control, or at least with less desire for control, less inter-ested in making wonders happen about us—or less able to. But the authors of the Bible refer to "the finger of God" (Exodus 8:19; Luke 11:20) and "the hand of the Lord" (1 Kings 18:46) to emphasize God's closeness with us and around us. Traditional interpretations of miracles sometimes explain these wonders—both in the pages of the Scriptures and since then, in the lives of the saints—as like new creations. According to most traditional teaching, a miracle is not simply something wonderful but also a new material creation, an altering of what otherwise would have happened.

One of the most common theological arguments against the existence of miracles today is that the New Testament age was a special time for wonders. According to this theory, the early church experienced a special outpouring of the Holy Spirit, as first described on the day of Pentecost in the book of Acts, that was not intended for all eras and all times. Many evangelical Protestant theologians, for instance, willingly accept the miracles of Scripture but not necessarily the miracles of the saints or of the church that are dated after the first century of Christianity.

(Pentecostal Protestants do not fit this generalization, as they emphasize miraculous "gifts" of the Holy Spirit, such as healing, speaking in tongues, and prophecy. This is why many non-Pentecostal Protestants regard Pentecostal practice in the same terms as they regard the miracles of Catholic saints. A televangelist urging ill viewers to place a trusting hand on the television set and a priest recommending devotion to St. Jude for those in dire need can seem very similar.)

Other Protestant theologians—in fact, most of them—are not interested in miracles today precisely because they do not accept the truth or accuracy of the miracles of Scripture. The rigors of seeking proof keep us from seeing what might be happening, and from believing what might be possible.

Catholic theologians argue that the church (its sacraments, its people) is the place of miraculous activity today, instituted by the Holy Spirit at Pentecost and exercised by Jesus and the first apostles. On this hinge of argument lies the usefulness of the saints in our spiritual lives today. They are lovely to think about, and their stories are charming to tell, but they can also be downright useful to us, if we believe. Do we believe that wonderworks can happen today, that miracles happen today?

Most Protestants, in the words of John Henry Newman from his *Essay on the Miracles,* believe "that Christianity is little more than a creed or doctrine, introduced into the world once for all, and then left to itself, after the manner of human institutions . . .

containing certain general promises of aid for this life, but unattended by any special divine Presence or any immediately supernatural gift." According to Newman, the early church fathers would have been shocked and disappointed to see that centuries after their teaching, "evidence would become a science," "doubt would be thought a merit, and disbelief a privilege."

The novelist David Guterson created a fictional account of miraculous apparitions of the Virgin Mary in a novel entitled *Our Lady of the Forest*. In the book, a sixteen-year-old runaway gathering food for herself in the woods of the Pacific Northwest stumbles upon "Our Lady." The story is a familiar one: as the girl's unexpected and completely unmerited visions intensify, crowds gather and the local religious leaders try to discredit her.

One reviewer of Guterson's novel began her review with these words, an admission of reader's guilt that could be extended to those of us who doubt more easily than we believe:

> We don't get many books about miracles any more, probably because we don't deserve them. Living in a world that recognizes only the palpable, we are poorly calibrated to register anything more delicate, or surprising. In part, this is because we are too egotistical to accept anything less than the empirical, acknowledging only the evidence of our own senses. Hierophany, the sacred made manifest, is a concession to this ideology of the obvious: that which passes understanding submits itself to our blunted powers of discernment.[10]

Perhaps Guterson's runaway-turned-saint could be any one of us.

Are we unable to see miracles because of our own lack of vision? Are we unable to believe in miracles chronicled by others because of our own imaginative deficiencies? Recent theologians have emphasized God's providence as entirely hidden, both before and after what we might point to as a miracle. According to this notion, miracles are actually remarkably common. Rather than rigorously question the veracity of someone who claims a divine vision, we might rather wonder aloud: "What is keeping me from experiencing something similar?" Or: "What is keeping me from realizing the wonderment all around me?" If the Spirit of God will help us, and our capacities for doing it are developed, we might be able to see things that we've never seen before.[11]

C. S. Lewis, the great British skeptic and professor of literature at Oxford, was intellectually convinced to convert to Christianity when his Catholic friend J. R. R. Tolkien said to him: "Your inability to picture for yourself the mysteries of Jesus' life is a failure of imagination on your part." We may need to accuse ourselves of the same failure.

Another intellectual of the past century, Simone Weil, argued that "if miracles possessed the nature, significance and value attributed to them [by Christ], their rarity today could induce the belief that the Church no longer had any part in God."[12] In other words, Jesus taught his disciples that any true believer would experience healings, casting out of devils, and signs of the Spirit. According to this measure, how many believers are there today?

In our own day, those who have visible religious experiences— the stigmatists and mystics—most closely resemble the "Jesus freaks" of a generation ago, or the young evangelical Christians of today. Just as most Catholic mystics—ancient, medieval, and modern—did not live out their twenties, today's young evangelicals who articulate a "radical" faith for Christ are almost always in their twenties or younger. Their faith is full of direct experience of God and is felt with deep emotion. Theirs is an authentic expression of relationship to God in Christ that is also a response to our rational age. And then, for some reason, that sort of passion and experience is outgrown.

The pathologies that skeptics find in today's evangelical faith are some of the same pathologies that skeptics, both religious and secular, have found in Catholic mystics through the ages. For example, whether you are "born again" or Thérèse of Lisieux, people are likely to view your avowed virginity and other forms of abstinence as a pathological condition, a sign of deep psychological trouble and avoidance, or as a sort of exhibitionism.

In conclusion, read these words of St. Bridget of Sweden, recorded after one of her visions. Bridget offers them as the words of Christ for her, and for us.

What you see you do not see as it really is, for if you saw the beauty of angels and holy souls your body could not bear the sight—it would burst asunder like a corrupt and rotten vessel with the joy your soul would feel. And indeed, if you saw devils as they really are you would either live with unbearable sorrow or die instantly at the fearful sight. And because of this, spiritual things are visible to you and shown in bodily likeness: angels in the likeness of men who have life and soul (for angels live in their spirits); devils are shown to you in the likeness of mortality, as beasts and other creatures without immortal souls (for when the flesh dies, the spirit dies, but in truth, devils are ever-dying and ever-living); spiritual ideas are conveyed to you through inner pictures, for the spirit could not otherwise apprehend them. And yet, among all these other things, the greatest marvel of all is that you feel my spirit moving in your heart.[13]

WHAT ABOUT THE MIRACLES OF JUSTICE?

One obstacle to wider appreciation of the saints is the incomplete picture that they sometimes seem to paint of the spiritual life. We shouldn't be satisfied with the simple, pious image of a saint. Whether male or female, saints are most commonly imaged waiting patiently on the Lord in prayer, in unflagging attention to devotion, in mystical union with God, in acts of humility, and in disregard for the things of the world. These are good things, but there is also more to a spiritual life.

Many of those outside the Catholic tradition have difficulty understanding and appreciating the contemplative vocation. In so many ways, more than ever before, we are a people of action, and when someone claims to be doing the work of God in private, we wonder how that is possible. It is more than possible, however, and the Christian tradition is rich with saints who lived contemplatively. Thomas Merton, the twentieth-century Trappist monk and popular spiritual writer, lived such a life. So did many other saints profiled in this book. In Merton's case, as he engaged more and more with the world outside the cloister walls—through his political writings and letters of encouragement to dissidents around the world during the 1960s—he felt God calling him to greater contemplation, silence, and distance from the noise of the world. Like the desert fathers and mothers centuries before them, modern contemplatives require silence and space. Often, they are today's prophets and most profound teachers. Even apart from what they may directly "give" to those of us in the world, they support us indirectly as well. You can imagine it this way: the prayers of the few support the inattention to prayer of the many.

We also want to see more miracles of justice, rather than simply miracles of the inexplicable. A clergy friend in Boston once explained to me the problem he had with the ministry of Mother Teresa. Imagine that you are living alongside a river, and babies in baskets are continually floating by. They are abandoned, sick, needy. You would try and care for the babies, wouldn't you? But wouldn't you also stop and say, "Where are all these babies coming from? How did they get here?" Social services, government agencies, religious groups, and saints are adept at finding babies, plucking them from the water, and helping them become well. But these same organizations—and saints like Mother Teresa—are not always focused enough on finding out who is putting all these babies in the river.

Mother Teresa was clearly a woman of action, but her efforts were almost entirely focused on compassionate response, not on attempting to slow or stop what was causing the enormous need. Much in her life is worthy of imitation, but we should also imitate those who perhaps do not possess the popular notion of sanctity but work hard to stop the politics, structures, policies, and institutions that make chronic hunger and disease possible.

Many saints have performed miracles of justice. We have profiled a number already: Oscar Romero, Thomas More, Dorothy Day, and Frances Cabrini, for example. Their miracles are focused entirely outside themselves; they are different from those who are saints of personality only, so to speak, and also different from someone like Mother Teresa, who avoided all political entanglements. Their lives show a commitment to peace, nonviolence, mediation, and justice for both the earth and all people and creatures. Daniel Berrigan, S.J., explains this perspective in an open letter he wrote in opposition to the cause for making Dorothy Day, his friend, a saint of the church:

> Abandon all thought of this expensive, overly juridical process. Let those so minded keep a photo of Dorothy some place given to prayer or worship. In such a place, implore her intercession for peace in the world, and bread for the multitudes.
>
> With the money thus saved, otherwise spent on ecclesiastical lawyers, expensive meetings and travel of experts, begin here and now feeding the multitudes. Send $1, $5, $10, $20, $100 to the nearest Catholic Worker house. Better still, drop by and help on the soup line. Best of all, start a Catholic Worker house.[14]

Berrigan asks all who would venerate Dorothy Day to imitate her instead. That is what she would have wanted most of all. At the same time, Berrigan acknowledges that this is how saints were originally made in the early church, by popular appeal. He explains that Dorothy is a saint already, interceding for peace in the world and for the rights and needs of the most needy; she doesn't need an ecclesiastical process to verify it.

Nikos Kazantzakis, in the prologue to the novel he wrote about the life of Francis of Assisi, summarized the meaning of Francis's life as a challenge to us. He wrote that we each have "the obligation to transubstantiate the matter which God entrusted to us, and turn it into spirit." Every Christian should show some heroic virtue and do the same.

Practices

Fr. Murray Bodo, O.F.M.

F<small>R. MURRAY BODO, O.F.M., IS A FRANCISCAN FRIAR</small>
and one of the most popular authors today of books
about Francis of Assisi (*Francis: the Journey and the
Dream, The Way of St. Francis, The Place We Call Home,* and
many others). Fr. Bodo is also a published poet and a frequent
leader of pilgrimage tours in Assisi. He writes, "I do have a relationship with two saints in particular—other than St. Francis, of
course: St. Thérèse of Lisieux and St. Clare of Assisi."

> St. Thérèse has been like a sister to me from the time I was
> a teenager at the high school seminary and read her *Story
> of a Soul* over and over again. Her childlike faith and her
> love of priests and those preparing for the priesthood was a
> great consolation to me. Her "little way" seemed something
> wholly doable to me then, something I could do to grow
> closer to Jesus. Also, her deep personal relationship with
> Jesus made her a model of what I wanted to become: a
> person in love with Jesus.
>
> I have prayed for her intercession for myself and others
> from the time I was fourteen years old and have experienced
> through her much spiritual consolation and the answer to
> many, many prayers. The following is a little meditation
> that may help you understand the effect of her spirituality
> on my life.

145

With Empty Hands

After earth's exile, I hope to go and enjoy you in the fatherland,

but I do not want to lay up merits for heaven.

I want to work for your love alone. . . . In the evening of this life,

I shall appear before you with empty hands, for I do not ask you,

Lord, to count my works. All our justice is blemished in your

eyes. I wish, then, to be clothed in your own justice and to receive

from your love the eternal possession of yourself (from *The Story of a Soul*).

In the end, all of us, like St. Thérèse of Lisieux, come before God with empty hands. We have nothing to boast of, as St. Paul says, except the cross of our Lord Jesus Christ, and yet we do not despair. For our very emptiness has made a space for God. If we have spent our lives loving God and others, there is a gradual self-emptying that becomes a filling up as well. We have nothing to offer but our empty hands—empty because they've surrendered all they've held on to—and those empty hands become the resting place of God.

Prayer of Surrender Inspired by St. Thérèse of Lisieux

Assume a position of prayer. Close your eyes and open your hands and surrender your life to God's mercy. You know what it is you need to surrender, but it is hard to let go of it. Don't be discouraged. The repeated handing over to God in prayer will work its own miracle.

One way to effect this surrender is to repeat, as a mantra, your deepest desire. For example, "God, my God, I want to be filled with you." After each uttering of this mantra, pause and let whatever objections, reservations, qualifications, excuses, etc., rise to the surface of your consciousness. Then resume: "God, my God, I want to be filled with you." Repeat this process for as long as your prayer time lasts.

What is important in this prayer is perseverance in the words and gestures of surrender. Real gestures such as opening your hands, or symbolic gestures of opening your soul, are both important. As St. Thérèse says succinctly in a letter to her sister Leonie, "I assure you that God is even kinder than you think. He is satisfied with a look, a sign of love."

St. Clare of Assisi is a more recent friend. I came to know her and her great gift of healing through the pilgrimages I have been making and leading to Assisi since 1976. One of our pilgrimage sites is the dormitory of St. Clare at San Damiano, outside the walls of Assisi. In 1978, while visiting her dormitory, we were interrupted by a commotion of Italians rushing up the narrow stairwell. A father held a boy in his arms who seemed to be in a coma. The crowd of people with him knelt as he laid the child on the floor on the exact spot where St. Clare had died. They all prayed briefly and then hurried off to the hospital in nearby Perugia.

We learned later that there had been a car accident, and the parents had insisted on bringing the boy to St. Clare for healing before rushing on to the hospital. We never learned what happened, but we were all moved by such faith and by the fact of St. Clare's healing gift. St. Francis and others used to send the sick to her for healing, and even today it is to St. Clare that many turn for healing of soul and body. I have personally seen spiritual and psychological healings, and the beginning of healings of addictions, effected through the services that we have included in our pilgrimages since the time of the incident of the young Italian boy.

In my own prayers for healing, I close my eyes and bring those for whom I am praying to the dormitory of St. Clare. I lay them on the floor where she died and leave them there with St. Clare to pray over as I watch in silence. At the end of the prayer, I open my eyes and release them.

PART THREE

Strange and Sublime

LIKE YOU, MY ADORABLE JESUS, I WANT TO BE scourged and crucified. I want to be flayed like St. Bartholomew. Like St. John, I want to be flung into boiling oil. Like St. Ignatius of Antioch, I long to be ground by the teeth of wild beasts, ground into a bread worthy of God. With St. Agnes and St. Cecelia, I want to offer my neck to the sword of the executioner and, like Joan of Arc, murmur the name of Jesus at the stake. My heart leaps when I think of the unheard tortures Christians will suffer in the reign of anti-Christ. I want to endure them all.

—St. Thérèse of Lisieux[1]

CHAPTER

9

The Stranger Side of Saintliness

SAINTS ARE STRANGE—THERE IS NO DENYING THAT— and if you did not grow up Catholic, they may seem even stranger. These pages have already mentioned many of the bizarre behaviors of the saints throughout history. Unusual behavior, in fact, in many ways defines sainthood. Typical, everyday Christians are saints in the broadest sense, but not in the official sense. Most of us lack the appropriate courage, vision, strength, compassion, and love that are found to an extraordinary degree in some of those set aside as having exhibited heroic virtue.

Three of the most befuddling aspects of sainthood are "the gift of tears," the seeming pleasure of pain, and foolishness aimed at holiness. Each of these unusual components of saintliness has a long history in the church and is seen as essential to the lives of many of our most loved saints in history. A fourth category, voluptuousness, actually encompasses the others, and although no saint would admit to striving for such a quality, we will see that many, in fact, have—and do.

TEARS

Lo where a Wounded Heart with Bleeding Eyes conspire.
Is she a Flaming Fountain, or a Weeping fire!

This odd couplet from the seventeenth-century English poet Richard Crashaw serves as an introduction to his poem "Saint Mary Magdalene, or The Weeper." Mary Magdalene is known for many things in Christian tradition, chief among them her witnessing to the apostles about the resurrection of Christ. When Mary first arrived at the tomb and saw that the stone had been removed from the entrance, she ran to Peter and John and told them that Jesus was no longer there. They all ran back to the spot, and once Peter and John saw for themselves, they quickly returned to their homes, presumably to tell the other disciples what had happened. But Mary remained at the tomb. The Gospel says that "Mary stood weeping outside the tomb" (John 20:11). Both angels and the resurrected Christ appeared to Mary there, and Jesus told her to go again to the disciples and witness to them that he had risen from the dead. She did.

Perhaps even more poignant, however, is that Mary Magdalene is often identified (mistakenly, according to most scholars) with the woman from Bethany—described as a sinner, probably a prostitute—who came to Jesus as he was dining with Simon the Pharisee and anointed Jesus' feet with tears and oil (Luke 7:36–50). Her tears wet his feet, and she used her long hair to wipe them clean. The Pharisees who were present found this very distasteful and criticized Jesus for allowing the woman to do it; Jesus explained it as the perfect expression of love.

(Novelist Dan Brown's recent worldwide best-selling novel, *The Da Vinci Code,* uses strands of theory that originated in the early Gnostic gospels to weave an intriguing story of Jesus and Mary Magdalene living as husband and wife after the Crucifixion. The novel tells a story of Mary and Jesus having a child together and the early church covering it up; it reveals Mary Magdalene to be the true "cup of Christ" of the Grail legends. Such theories, it should be pointed out, are doubted by every serious scholar of early Christianity.)

Whether or not Mary Magdalene was the woman who adored Jesus' feet with tears of sorrow and repentance, the image of the woman from Bethany remains one of the most powerful in the New Testament. The tears that the prodigal son probably shed—upon seeing the look of total forgiveness on his father's face—might compare, but not quite. Men, in particular, have made much over the centuries of the Bethany woman's repentance for carnal sin, but the nature of the sin is irrelevant to the experience of repentance, shown so beautifully in her actions before Christ that day.

In his poem to "The Weeper," Crashaw writes as if he is praying to Mary Magdalene, and his reflections demonstrate the perceived value of tears in saints, and in the pious:

> Upwards thou dost weep.
> Heaven's bosom drinks the gentle stream,
> Where the milky rivers creep,
> Thine floats above; & is the cream.
> Waters above the Heavens, what they be
> We are taught best by thy Tears & thee.

Crashaw's praising of tears goes further, and we see the reasoning behind them. For the saint, it is God's "well-pointed dart" piercing and wounding the human heart that "digged these wells" for tears. The wounded heart of the saint is likened to a fire of passion for God. "Fair floods" of tears are then the "friends" of "the bosom fires that fill thee." These two elements— a fiery passion for God and tearful outward expressions of love for God—mark the life of a saint who is specially gifted in this way.

> O floods, o fires! o suns o showers!
> Mixed & made friends by love's sweet powers.

Consider also the tears of Mary the mother of Jesus at the foot of the cross on Calvary. She was standing "nearby looking on" as her son died, according to tradition. The four Gospels disagree as to which women were there at Calvary, but John's Gospel clearly states, "[S]tanding near the cross of Jesus were his mother, and his mother's sister, Mary the wife of Clopas, and Mary Magdalene" (John 19:25). While there is no specific mention of tears in the Gospel accounts, they were surely an important feature of what was happening there, at Christ's death and until after the Resurrection. Mary's tears, and saintly tears in general, are also often prefigured in the lamentations of the prophet Jeremiah for the people of Israel. Tears were prescribed by the prophet as an essential step toward redemption.

> Thus says the LORD of hosts:
> Consider, and call for the mourning women to come;
>> send for the skilled women to come;
> let them quickly raise a dirge over us,
>> so that our eyes may run down with tears,
>> and our eyelids flow with water.
> (Jeremiah 9:17-18)

Mary's heart is understood to have an enormous capacity for love, care, and passion for God. In the symbolism of Catholic devotion, Mary's heart is second only to the Sacred Heart of Jesus.

Even the intellectual skeptic Simone Weil understood "the gift of tears," as it is known in Catholic tradition, to be real:

> One man weeps with physical pain; another by the side of him weeps for thinking about God with a pure love. In both cases there are tears. These tears are the results produced by a psycho-physical mechanism. But in one of the two cases a wheel of this mechanism is a supernatural one; it is charity. In this sense, although tears are such an ordinary phenomenon, the tears of a saint in a state of genuine contemplation are supernatural.[1]

The connection between sorrow and faith that is present in the tears of a saint is distinctive of women in the history of Christianity. Male saints have occasionally experienced the gift, as well, and Ignatius of Loyola was known to have recommended to other men that they, too, ask the Lord for the gift of tears. Still, the two Marys remain supreme examples.

PAIN

One of the most famous images of a saint is Gian Lorenzo Bernini's marble statue of Teresa of Avila in the Cornaro Chapel of Santa Maria della Vittoria, in Rome. Teresa appears close to death as a spear pierces her heart and she begins to writhe. The angel who delivers the heavenly stabs smiles gently over Teresa, obviously pleased to be able to give them to her. One writer has called the famous sculpture "art's most convincing orgasm."[2]

Bernini didn't create the sculpture purely out of his imagination; it was inspired by Teresa's own writing. A matter-of-fact and businesslike woman, Teresa was nevertheless forced by one of her confessors to write down her religious experiences. Explaining that this particular vision was representative of others but also that she was not accustomed to seeing angels standing before her, Teresa wrote:

> In his hands I saw a long golden spear and at the end of the iron tip I seemed to see a point of fire. With this he seemed to pierce my heart several times so that it penetrated to my entrails. When he drew it out, I thought he was drawing them out with it and he left me completely afire with a great love for God. The pain was so sharp that it made me utter several moans; and so excessive was the sweetness caused me by this intense pain that one can never wish to lose it.[3]

Bernini's sculpture—and perhaps Teresa's experience—was intended to show that there is an ecstasy that is divine and that means far more than sex ever could (see chapter ten for more on this). Teresa was one of the wittiest and funniest religious women in history, but she also experienced a closeness with God, a love for God, that involved pain.

Saints have glorified pain as both a responsibility of the godly and a gift from God. St. Margaret of Cortona once said, "I want to die of starvation in order to satiate the poor." St. Gemma Galgani, a modern saint (she died of tuberculosis in 1903), suffered flamboyantly and inspired many priests, confessors, and psychologists alike to investigate her for either saintliness or hysteria that should be treated with medicine or therapy. Gemma believed that Jesus was often saying to her: "My works of love on the cross, the scourging, blood, and inhuman pain, are yours to emulate, if you will love me in return."[4]

Very few Christians today would see the sense in such a glorification of suffering, but Gerard Manley Hopkins, the Christian mystical poet, offers a helpful explanation of how pain and joy can blend together in the spirituality of remembering Christ's passion. In a commentary on his well-known poem "The Wreck of the Deutschland," Hopkins explains: "It is the heart in extremity which best understands and proclaims the beauty and terror of that Sacrifice. Some are forced to cry 'How bitter!' Others taste only the sweetness. But, sour or sweet, the result is overwhelming conviction."[5]

FOOLISHNESS

History and literature are replete with stories of saints' holy foolishness. Fyodor Dostoevsky's classic novel *The Idiot,* for example, portrays an antihero, Prince Myshkin, who never finds fault in others and is kind, generous, and, well, saintly—to the point of foolishness. Throughout the novel, Myshkin speaks his mind in his utmost simplicity and without regard for how his words might sound to others. He is seemingly unable to conspire or scheme, unlike the cleverer people around him. He shares of himself and his inheritance in ways that seem unwise to more-worldly people. And he loves too unboundedly, as seen in this scene, where he is trying to convince the woman he loves that he will love her rightly and more purely than the other characters in the novel, who do not have her interests in mind.

> "I'll take you as an honest woman, Nastasya Filippovna, not as Rogozhin's kind," said the prince.
>
> "Me, an honest woman?"
>
> "You."
>
> "Well, that's . . . out of some novel! That, my darling prince, is old gibberish, the world's grown smarter now, and that's all nonsense! And how can you go getting married, when you still need a nursemaid to look after you!"
>
> The prince stood up and said in a trembling voice, but with a look of deep conviction:
>
> "I don't know anything, Nastasya Filippovna. . . . I . . . love you. . . . I will die for you. . . . I won't let anyone say a bad word about you."

The other characters in the novel, both the men and the women, scoff at pronouncements such as these. "He is an idiot," they say. Or: "He is raving mad." "What a kind man!" one woman exclaims, while another character responds: "A cultivated man, but a lost one!"[6]

A fool and a saint are not to be admired in our world. The world dismisses him, or scoffs at her, saying something like, "He is either for God alone—and of what use in society is that?—or he is actually selfishly for himself alone, and how are we to discern the difference?"

Is it impossible to thrive in the secular world and still be a saint? Prince Myshkin clearly cannot succeed at both. He is the genuine article, not someone trying to be a saint, but a man in whom saintly virtues already abound and exude themselves effortlessly; Myshkin cannot help this, and he suffers for it. He is Dostoevsky's ideal of a man, modeled after Christ's example of combining the human and the spiritual in one. Dostoevsky seemed to struggle his whole life with the idea of whether or not such a person could actually exist, let alone survive. His character Myshkin obviously cannot survive in the "real" world of greed, corruption, intrigue, and lies. He is too simple and too full of faith.

Dostoevsky once wrote that his intent in *The Idiot* was "to portray a perfectly beautiful man." He ultimately concluded that the experiment to create a saint was a failure:

> The beautiful is an ideal, but this ideal . . . is still far from being worked out. There is only one perfectly beautiful person—Christ—so that the appearance of this immeasurably, infinitely beautiful person is, of course, already an infinite miracle. (That is the sense of the whole Gospel of John: it finds the whole miracle in the incarnation alone, in the manifestation of the beautiful alone.)[7]

Plenty of fools exist in Christian tradition. St. Joseph of Cupertino (d. 1663) was a Franciscan whose behavior would have likely gone unappreciated, or at least been misunderstood, by Francis of Assisi himself. The two men are excellent examples of the differences between holy foolishness that might land someone in a mental hospital and holy foolishness that is part of a strategy of ministry. St. Francis often engaged in the latter; he played the fool himself, at times with his spiritual brothers, in order to demonstrate his love for God and relative disregard for the values of the world (decorum, property, honor). Francis liked to think of himself and his first friars as "God's jugglers" who would travel from village to village in Italy and elsewhere entertaining people with the Good News. The earliest Franciscans begged for their bread, often slept outdoors, and spent a lot of time with lepers, who at that time were complete outcasts of society, including the church. In those days, such actions were deemed bizarre, and the children of the villages would often throw mud and rocks at the "crazy friars," regarding them to be as low on the social scale as vagabond lunatics. For Francis, however, deliberate simplicity had a purpose in ministry. He and the first Franciscans were aiming to distinguish themselves clearly from the institutional church and the wealthy religious orders of their day. As a result, so many men and women soon wanted to join Francis that he was forced to create what he called the "Third order," giving laypeople a way to join the spirit and efforts of the Franciscan movement without leaving family, job, or community.

Joseph of Cupertino, on the other hand, was known to have psychological problems—or unusual, mysterious private mystical experiences, depending on your perspective. He is known in history as the "flying friar" because he was reported to have levitated on many occasions. Many of his contemporaries attested to these flights, or simple risings into the air, including those who tried to bat him back down to earth, disgusted by what they interpreted as attention-craving foolishness. Levitations, in fact, are a little-known aspect of the bizarre side of saintliness. The skeptical writer V. Sackville-West, in her dual biography of Sts. Teresa of Avila and Thérèse of Lisieux, writes: "The Rev. Herbert Thurston, S.J., most cautious and skeptical of investigators, personally described to the present writer the case of a priest of his acquaintance, who was obliged to weight the soles of his boots with lead in order to keep himself down while saying Mass. But, as Father Thurston remarked, it did seem puzzling that a little extra weight should make all that difference to a supernatural power capable of lifting a man's body without any difficulty."[8]

Although by most accounts Joseph of Cupertino was unable to accomplish even the simplest tasks as a young boy, and later had very little to contribute as a lay brother in his order, and surely could not read, write, or even comprehend much of the Scriptures, he was somehow ordained a priest in 1628. After that time, his life seems to have been occupied with bizarre behavior. He was recorded to have levitated in the air at least seventy times, and his various stupors were often interpreted to be ecstatic trances, which left him unable to speak or move. After Joseph's death, his cult sprang up almost immediately; pilgrims began to gather at his tomb in Osimo, Italy, and report miracles of healing there. Canonized one hundred years after his death, largely due to public demand, Joseph of Cupertino is an example of a man who was undoubtedly challenged in many ways psychologically but is remembered for his humility and gentleness—and the miracles attributed to his intercession. His cult centers on his radical simplicity, which is still seen today as an antidote to spiritual practice that is too much concerned with worldly power and influence.

Many of the Orthodox saints of the eighteenth and nineteenth centuries are also among the most delightful of the "holy fools" of the Christian tradition. We must at least briefly mention the Russian saint Seraphim of Sarov, who has exemplified a more approachable and reasonable form of holy foolishness for many Orthodox Christians since his life and death in the early nineteenth century.

Seraphim loved to be alone, and he also loved to practice austerities. He used a bag of stones as a pillow and even carried the bag with him from place to place, as if it was something valuable. Even as an old man in his seventies living alone in the forest, Seraphim had the spirit of a child, and children and adults came as pilgrims from faraway places to meet him. His face showed bliss and joy, and it was common to see him playing with some wild creature, including a bear that he would pet as if it was a lamb.

VOLUPTUOUSNESS

I was never made for understanding this "union with God" business: St. Teresa and the rest. I don't know what it is all about and the description of isolation and detachment,

"the necessary night of the soul," disgusts me like Wagner's music or boiled mutton. Good for others: not for me.
—Hilaire Belloc

Hilaire Belloc, a popular English Catholic writer of the early twentieth century, was just as confused about the stranger side of saintliness as are many of us today.

It was Friedrich Nietzsche, I think, who first used the word *voluptuous* to describe saints, and he did not mean it as a compliment. He wanted to make clear the extravagance and misplaced eroticism of some saintly behavior. When a saint is mystically "wed" to Christ, Nietzsche believed, it is not a means of submission to God and abstaining from worldly things. It is instead a way of gaining power over other people. In today's age, when we are very much aware of the abuse of clerical power, it is not difficult to see his point.

Modern lives of the saints now sometimes use the word *voluptuous* to describe holy behaviors that seem too full of affect. Louise Collis, for instance, in her lovely life of Margery Kempe, says: "[S]he felt God preferred meditation rather than the repetition of set prayers. 'Ihesu,' she sighed voluptuously, 'what schal I thynke?' 'Thynke on my Modyr,' he replied."[9]

Other critics in recent centuries have argued that the extravagance of the saints is a kind of cowardice. Like Scarlett O'Hara's strategic use of emotion in *Gone with the Wind,* the saints may use similar tactics as they confront the realities of life. E. M. Cioran wrote:

> Swooning saints have a moving charm. They prove that we cannot have revelations in a vertical position, that we cannot stand on our feet to face the ultimate truth. Swooning provokes such wild voluptuousness that a man cognizant of negative joys has a hard time deciding whether to fall or not.[10]

Religious women are not the only ones to have taken Christ as their spouse, but it is most common. The legends of women saints, and their writings, are full of erotic images of union with Christ substituting for consummation with a husband, which was expected of every woman throughout the Middle Ages. Following Christ's advice to the first disciples in

160

Luke 14:26, "Whoever comes to me and does not hate father and mother, wife and children, brothers and sisters . . . cannot be my disciple," some of these medieval saints were radical in their wishes. Both Angela of Foligno and Bridget of Sweden, for instance, openly wished to be freed from loving family relationships in order to follow Christ as completely as they desired. St. Bridget, in fact, prayed earnestly to God: "Rip the thorn which is in my heart, which is bodily love for my husband or children or friends or relatives."[11] Angela of Foligno thanked God upon the death of her husband and children.

Angela was voluptuously saintly. After her conversion, she wanted nothing more than to become a full-time Franciscan tertiary. She believed that she was following Christ, who had said to his own mother: "Get away from me." She had her oddities chronicled to demonstrate the extravagance of her holy intentions. She was known to disregard herself to great extremes. Not only did Angela have visions and forget to eat when she was intoxicated with joy, but she was also known to care for lepers, which was not uncommon for Franciscans, but she took her carelessness for her own health to an extreme by partaking of the lepers' sores as one would the host of Christ.

Angela also called out involuntarily. For a time, early in the days of her conversion, whenever she heard people speaking of God she would cry out. She used plenty of erotic imagery to describe her relationship with Christ. She focused her attention on the wounds of Christ in meditation, for example, and became so enraptured with them that she imagined herself with her mouth on his side, "drinking and being purified by the blood flowing from it."

She once implored St. Francis, who was her patron saint, to intercede with God on her behalf so that she might "feel Christ." In a dramatic vision, Angela was wed to God, who told her, "You have my ring of love." She was in such a state of ecstasy afterward that she was reported to be immovable for eight days.

Other visions Angela had took her even deeper into this sort of relationship with Jesus. Her ultimate vision of intimacy with Christ her betrothed was one in which she vividly saw herself identifying with the crucified Jesus by lying with him in the grave. "With eyes closed as He lay there dead, a wondrous odor coming from His mouth as she kissed it. She placed her cheek against His and Christ placed a hand on her other cheek to press her close," wrote the narrator of all of Angela's experiences, Arnaldo, her confessor and a Franciscan friar.

In Angela's nineteenth step toward God (she counted thirty in these dictated memoirs), she describes God's "sweetness" and her desire to sell everything, leave behind all friends and family, and have only Christ.

Because it is so closely associated with desiring attention, voluptuousness is often disregarded as a mark of saintliness that should be admired and possibly imitated. But the countercultural quality of these actions can still instruct us, especially today. Sometimes the defining marks of faith put us in opposition to cultural norms and expectations, and the voluptuous saints stand to remind us dramatically of this truth.

Practices

Br. Wayne Teasdale

B R. WAYNE TEASDALE WAS A LAY MONK WHO, UNTIL recently, lived in Chicago and taught at the Catholic Theological Union and DePaul University. He passed away in the autumn of 2004. A close friend and student of His Holiness the Dalai Lama and the late Bede Griffiths, Br. Wayne was the author of several books, including *A Monk in the World, The Mystic Heart,* and *Bede Griffiths: An Introduction to His Interspiritual Thought.*

I have a personal relationship with a number of saints, but the most long-lasting relationship I have with a saint is with St. Francis of Assisi. My relationship with Francis began in my childhood when I read several books about him, and St. Clare as well. What brought me into relationship with Francis was the experience of being inspired by his example in reading his life, the stories about his holiness,

163

his gift for prayer, and his connectedness with nature, animals, birds, and other human beings. This particular saint stood out for me, and he managed to capture my heart and my imagination. I wanted to be just like him, and I strove so to be.

I have to say: Francis is one of my best friends, and I feel I know him, and have known him since I was a child.

I have developed what I call "the practice of nature," and it was St. Francis who inspired me to do so. It involves a vigorous walk of up to an hour in the midst of the natural world in which you are emptying your mind of everything and, like Francis, are connecting consciously with all that you are aware of: the trees, birds, clouds, seagulls, dogs, and persons passing, the wind blowing in your face and among the trees.

CHAPTER 10

The Love of a Woman

WHY IS THERE NOTHING IN THE BIBLE THAT tells a Christian how exactly to love an invisible God? The Bible tells us: "You shall love the Lord your God with all your heart, and with all your soul, and with all your mind" (Matthew 22:37). But how are we to do this?

The traditional Protestant response to Jesus' command to love is confusing at times. It can sometimes seem that we believe willpower alone will bring about the desired results. If we are not loving enough toward spouse, neighbor, or God, we should try harder, perhaps asking God for the strength to do it, as if loving were a state of mind.

The devotions to the saints and other ancient Christian practices offer tangible experiments in loving. The capacity to love is something that we can develop through practice, which should then result in making us better lovers—of God and one another. As many of the women saints in history have shown and taught, there are various ways of loving God, of approaching God in devotion, friendship, and intimacy, just as

God approaches us. These ideas cut straight to the heart of medieval faith, in which the most basic question in the world, "Why did God create?" has the most beautiful answer: "Because Love can do no other."

Some of the saints' teachings and examples of how to love God in Christ are bewildering to us today, and some of the women saints, in particular, use even shocking images for loving God. We glimpsed some of these teachings and examples in the previous chapter. Still, as these women offer us ways to know God more intimately, even the folly of their lives is worth understanding. As Silvius says to the jaded Corin in Shakespeare's *As You Like It:* "If thou remember'st not the slightest folly / That ever love did make thee run into, / Thou hast not loved."

CHRIST THE MARRIAGE PARTNER

The exemplary women of Christian tradition are not always what they may at first seem—meek, quiet, and endlessly forgiving, like those deeply ingrained images and legends surrounding the Virgin Mary that we have discussed. St. Helena was an explorer and a woman of tremendous courage. St. Teresa of Avila was as good an administrator and church leader as any person before or since her time. St. Joan of Arc was a soldier, a militant, a person with whom you would trust your very life. Many women saints have also been great and extravagant lovers—lovers of God in Christ.

There is a rich tradition of women saints who are focused on the love of God—or, more precisely, the love of Christ. Their lives and teachings offer hints of what is possible to those of us who are sometimes at a loss as to how to deepen our divine connections. In the lives of these fascinating women—who were most prominent between the late medieval period (thirteenth to fourteenth centuries) and the beginning of our modern era (nineteenth to early twentieth centuries)—love of Christ can sometimes sound a lot like erotic love, but this should really be of no surprise to us. The Song of Songs, that enigmatic Scripture that has been a model for divine intimacy for millennia in both Jewish and Christian mysticism, is full of erotic imagery. Monastic writers and celibates such as Bernard of Clairvaux (who spent almost eighteen years of his life exploring the Song of Songs) have written verse-by-verse commentaries of the text, offering allegorical interpretations of how the intimacy between a man and a woman can mirror the intimacy between God and human. Seraphim of Sarov taught his students that God is like fire in the body, and love of God heats you up, whereas the devil makes you cold.

Women saints have for centuries consciously exchanged their natural ability for sex and childbirth for a union sanctified with Christ alone, birthing divine possibilities in themselves and others rather than babies. Thérèse of Lisieux wrote in her letters: "I think that the Heart of my Spouse is mine alone, just as mine is His alone, and I speak to Him then in the solitude of this delightful heart to heart, while waiting to contemplate Him one day face to face."[1] In one of her poems, she calls Christ her "Supreme Beauty" and pines, "For you I must die." In another, she explains that "the kiss of his mouth"—that of her lover, Christ—bestows on her the treasures of purity, chastity, and virginity. This reference, and many others in Thérèse's poems, is to the Song of Songs. Mechtild of Magdeburg (d. ca. 1297) writes longingly in the first part of *The Flowing Light of the Godhead,* a recording of her visions: "Ah Lord! love me greatly, love me often and long! For the more continuously Thou loves me, the purer I shall be. The more fervently Thou loves me, the more lovely I shall be. The longer Thou loves me the more holy I shall become, even here on earth." These images have the power to shock us, but they also make sense.

Some critics will point out, however, that this focus on feminine life and love apart from body and sex is only the result of a lack of real choices. Until very recently, much of the religious world was caught up in the notion of a world marked by the combat of good (spirit) and evil (body). Women, in particular, were constrained to do with their bodies only what their fathers, husbands, or priests (who were always men) permitted them to do. Critics will argue that this is often what fueled women to become saints, so that they might "conceive" Christ through self-denial in abbeys and through penitence as a way of creating meaningful, even though incomplete, life. These trends surely existed in the medieval mind-set and in its attitudes toward the role of women—and still do, perhaps, in the most conservative branches of Christianity and Islam today. But there is far more positive than negative in this story.

Sexually charged language of uncertainty and desire and unusual and ambiguous relationships were also features of religious life centuries ago that today are nothing new. Consider the case of Christina of Markyate (d. 1161), an Anglo-Saxon girl who desired to preserve her virginity forever and devote her life to serving God. Her parents would have nothing of it, and neither would most of the church. Apparently, Christina was lovely and had a remarkable sexual attractiveness to men; there also is some evidence that she herself was sexually drawn to men merely by sight. The gorgeous Christina dreamed of bulls chasing her, had encounters with men who exposed themselves to her, felt eros so great "that she thought the clothes which clung to her body might be set on fire," and scourged herself alone in her room in the evenings to expel these desires of the flesh. She repelled all advances throughout her charged life, even violent ones from her pursuers, and the advances of her own heart.

Even then, it was another saint who came to help Christina. Mary Magdalene appeared to Christina's pursuer in a dream, glaring at him "with piercing eyes." Mary

> reproached him harshly for his wicked persecution of the chosen spouse of the most high king. [Christina had betrothed herself to Christ.] And at the same time she threatened him that if he troubled her any further, he would not escape the anger of almighty God and eternal damnation. Terrified at the vision and awakened from sleep, he went to the maiden in a changed mood and, revealing to her what he had seen and heard, begged and obtained her pardon.[2]

It is good to remember that, down through the centuries, most of the stories of the saints were recorded by men, and the abundance of tales of women trying to overcome sexual desires most likely stem from the less-than-holy visions of these scribes. The legends of many other women may be, in large part, the creation of men. St. Mary of Egypt, for instance, a former prostitute, was believed to have made her way to the desert and lived among the solitary monks there, tempting them with her beauty and reputation. And St. Veronica, believed by some in the Middle Ages to have been the daughter of Salome, the sexy dancer who was the stepdaughter of King Herod and at whose request John the Baptist was beheaded, stepped out of the crowd as Jesus made his way to Golgotha and offered a cloth on which he wiped his face.

The intimate descriptions of women's experience of Jesus as a marriage partner, however, do not fit this category. These were recorded not by men with questionable intentions but by the women themselves. The intimacy of these narratives is unnerving to those of us standing on the outside. It is as if these women were chosen for betrothal personally by God, and the intimacy they develop is very special.

For example, in Ron Hansen's novel *Mariette in Ecstasy,* Mariette Baptiste is a simple woman who asks to be received into the Sisters of the Crucifixion. The character is based on many real examples in history of women mystics who were either grossly misunderstood or beside themselves. In the final chapters of Hansen's best-selling novel, Mariette experiences and tries to explain her mystical communion with Jesus and is greeted only with greater and greater suspicion by her sisters, and was even put in prison. In the climax of the book, Mariette is interrogated about her experiences, even as she is having them:

"Where are you?" Sister Philomène whispers.
"Sitting in choir," she says, "with the Psalter."
"And is Jesus there?"
"Yes."
Sister Léocadie asks, "Oh, what does he look like?"
"Handsome," she says. . . .
She tells them, "He holds my hand in his and we two walk down the hallway to his house inside ours. Which is his heart." . . .
"What else?" Sister Léocadie asks.
Mariette thinks for a little while and says, "We are alone. We touch each other, but he withdraws. 'You are unclean,' he says, and I am ashamed because I see that it's true. Every sin I have committed is written in ink on my skin. Christ tells me to undress. And then he gently washes me with his hands." . . .

169

> She kneels just in front of the frowning prioress. . . .
> "And he gives me food as I have never eaten. And fine wine
> from a jeweled chalice. When he tells me to sleep, I do so
> at once, and he holds me. And I share in him as if he's
> inside me. And he is."[3]

This sort of imagery is to be found throughout the writings
and the lives of women saints. It is most commonly an experience that women have had of God, however; very few men have
known this sort of intimacy with Christ firsthand. Meister
Eckhart and other male mystics speak often of union with God
(Eckhart preached that the real meaning of Christmas is the birth
of God in the human soul) but never through the intimate
metaphor of bride and bridegroom. One notable exception,
however, is Juan de Yepes, or St. John of the Cross (d. 1591), a
Spanish Carmelite priest who was spiritual adviser to Teresa of
Avila. Like an anchorite, John spent many hours in seclusion,
often in prison (he was accused by other Carmelites of trying
to subvert their authority with his reforms of the order).
Among his writings is a series of poems called "The Spiritual
Canticle." Recalling his first union with Christ—in the voice of
a bride speaking to her bridegroom—John writes in the first
stanza:

> Where are you hiding,
> Beloved, that I am left moaning?
> You fled like a stag,
> leaving me here wounded;
> I have called for you, but no answer.

Eroticism in the lives of women saints was often shocking
even to them. Teresa of Avila's ecstasy, which she hesitantly
shared in her autobiography and was then immortalized in
sculpture (Bernini's marble statue in the Cornaro Chapel in
Rome) and poetry, was for Teresa a very private affair. She
was, to those who knew her, as businesslike as she could be. One
writer explains the contrast this way, with enthusiasm: "Never,
never, it cannot be over-emphasized, did any mystic more profoundly mistrust such seizures than this sane, vigorous, intelligent,
humorous Spaniard, or lose fewer opportunities of warning
other people against them."[4]

Some scholars have compared the courtly literature of the Middle Ages—love notes from gallant troubadours to unapproachable ladies—with mystical writings of love such as those found in the Song of Songs and other Wisdom Literature and in the memoirs and visions of women saints. It is true that the two genres—mystical writings and courtly literature—seemed to originate and flourish at about the same time, and in both cases the expressions of love are feeble compared to the reality of love that is possible. But the love of a troubadour for a fair lady is often poignant because it is unrequited, and more beautiful in its expression because of the pain that accompanies such strong passion in the midst of daily strife and courage. For the women saints, on the other hand, intimacy and love was deeply imagined, experienced, and described. It is poignant precisely because it is requited by God, who is Love itself, and it has everything to do with daily strife, as it intentionally brings Christian theology full circle. Don't look to understand it, however, with the head and not the body. John of the Cross explains in his prologue to "The Spiritual Canticle":

> Who can describe in writing the understanding he gives to loving souls in whom he dwells? And who can express with words the experience he imparts to them? Who, finally, can explain the desires he gives them? Certainly, no one can! Not even they who receive these communications. As a result [they] let something of their experience overflow in figures, comparisons and similitudes, and from the abundance of their spirit pour out secrets and mysteries rather than rational explanations.[5]

Mystical love for God, expressed in often uncomfortable and naturalistic bodily terms, is an answer to why the fall of humanity ever had to occur, how God acts primarily within us in the world today, and how heaven is not primarily a future promise or threat but a reality here and now in the hearts of those who will allow it to be and grow. Julia Kristeva, an intelligent observer, explains: "[Saints] impart willpower to their love, enlighten it with reason, tinge it with wisdom, in order to raise it to the dignity of a divine essence."[6] The birth of God in us is a fully redeemed life. As a monk friend of mine likes to say when giving retreats to Protestant

171

groups, "The redemption of you is much more than your salvation. Your body is redeemed as well!"

CHRIST OUR MOTHER

There is a deeper relationship to God in Christ than that of a lover. One of the great women saints has also shown us how Christ is our Mother.

Julian of Norwich (d. ca. 1420) brings us to a new understanding of the love of God, the intimacy of the love of God, and how we may truly experience it when we embrace God in the feminine. Julian is recognized as a saint in the Anglican (Episcopal) tradition, and she is traditionally called a Blessed in Catholicism. She introduces us to the Motherhood of Jesus, what she calls "the Motherhood of mercy and grace." This, too, has its origins in the Wisdom Literature of the Bible, in which God, All-Wisdom, is clearly identified with the feminine. Julian explains:

> We know that our mothers bring us into the world with suffering and that we suffer and die. But our True Mother, Jesus, he—All-Love—bears us to joy and endless life. Blessed be he! He sustains us within himself in love and labored to full term until he suffered the sharpest pains and the most grievous sufferings that ever were or ever shall be. . . . And when he finished and he had born us to bliss, even this could not fully satisfy his marvelous love. . . . So next it moved him to feed us. . . . [O]ur dear Mother, Jesus, can feed us with himself and does it, tenderly. . . . With the sweet sacraments he sustains us most mercifully and most graciously.

Christ is our Mother in nature, a result of the Incarnation, and in spirit, as we find all spiritual nourishment in Christ. Christ becomes the deepest well for our cares. We are knit with Christ, All-Wisdom, who in Julian's words nurtures his children, allowing them to learn lessons and encounter hardships but without ever allowing us to stop feeling his deep, abiding love. We are of one substance with Christ our Mother, just as we are one person with Christ our Bridegroom.

Julian refers to God as "the Creator, the Keeper, the Lover" and adds: "Until I am substantially one with him I may never have full rest nor true bliss. That is to say, until I be so fastened to him that there is nothing that is made between my God and me."

These two intimacies—of God as lover and marriage partner and of God as mother—offer us new ways (that are not so new) to know God in Christ. "It is God's will that every soul should reflect inwardly on its Love," says Julian.[7] Let us do that. Our bodies become places where holiness happens. God with us becomes God in us. What a challenge to live up to that reality! It is no wonder, then, that the magnificent women saints of our traditions often thought little of the health and welfare of their bodies, as their intimacies with Christ had them already in heaven.

Practices

Celebrating the Feasts of the Saints

THROUGHOUT THE WORLDWIDE CHURCH, SPECIAL days known as feast days are set aside for remembering and honoring one or more of the saints. A feast day is usually the day recognized as the saint's birthday in heaven, or day of new life—in other words, the day he or she died on earth. A feast day is primarily a liturgical celebration, but one may also use private prayers and remembrances found in the devotional books of many traditions on these special days.

October 4 is always highlighted on my calendar, as it is the feast day of St. Francis of Assisi, my patron saint. I usually give a talk about his life and spiritual vitality in church on that day, and I love participating in the "Blessing of the Animals" that we also celebrate on that day (or on the Sunday closest to October 4).

The beauty and pageantry of public feast-day celebrations are often greatest in predominantly Catholic countries or communities, although Anglicans (Episcopalians) and mainline Lutherans also commemorate saints on special days. All Saints'

175

Day—celebrated in Western churches on November 1 and in the Eastern churches on the first Sunday after Pentecost—is also recognized in various other denominations around the world.

In Brazil, millions of people fill the streets each October for a procession to honor *Nossa Senhora de Aparecida* (Our Lady Who Appeared). This is known as Mary's Day, and there are many other feasts and festivals on the calendar in Brazil to celebrate other saints. People shed their shoes, carry handmade crosses and images of the saint, and thank God for blessings given, all while dancing in celebration, and while fireworks are displayed overhead.

I don't expect that the average Protestant family in America will have as much fun as families do in Brazil on a saint's feast day, but it can be meaningful for families to celebrate a saint's feast day together. Choose a saint as patron of your family and learn about him or her. Find a popular image or icon of your saint and talk together about the symbolism in the depiction. Ask the children and perhaps even extended family members to participate by each researching some aspect of the person's life. On the actual day, create a home celebration. You may even want to make this special day each year the anniversary of a beloved grandparent's death, celebrating his or her birth into the communion of saints in heaven.

The following dates represent selected annual celebrations in both the Western and Eastern churches for some of the saints discussed in detail throughout this book. When the name for the feast differs in the churches, the Eastern name is given in parentheses, but in all cases, the date given for the feast is according to the Roman calendar (of the West).

January 2	Basil the Great and Gregory Nazianzen
January 17	Antony of Egypt
January 24	Francis de Sales
January 28	Thomas Aquinas
February 23	Polycarp
March 3	Katharine Drexel (on U.S. calendar only)
March 17	Patrick
March 25	The Annunciation
April 4	Isidore of Seville

April 29	Catherine of Siena
May 25	Venerable Bede
June 29	Peter and Paul (jointly)
July 11	Benedict of Nursia
July 22	Mary Magdalene
July 23	Bridget of Sweden
July 31	Ignatius of Loyola
August 11	Clare of Assisi
August 15	The Assumption of Mary (The Dormition of Our Lady)
August 20	Bernard of Clairvaux
August 28	Augustine of Hippo
August 29	John the Baptist
September 8	Birth of Mary
September 29	Michael, Gabriel, and Raphael (jointly)
September 30	Jerome
October 1	Thérèse of Lisieux
October 4	Francis of Assisi
October 15	Teresa of Ávila
November 1	All Saints' Day
November 13	Frances Xavier Cabrini (on U.S. calendar only)
November 16	Margaret of Scotland
November 17	Elizabeth of Hungary
December 13	Lucia
December 14	John of the Cross
December 28	The Holy Innocents
December 29	Thomas à Becket

Three Prayers for Use on Any Feast Day

The following prayers are slight variations on three prayers in common use throughout Christian churches on the feast days of saints. These versions closely resemble those found in the Episcopal Book of Common Prayer (the current [1979] edition).

O Almighty God, who has compassed us about with so great a cloud of witnesses: Grant that we, encouraged by the good example of thy servant _____, may persevere in running the race that is set before us, until at length, through thy mercy, we may with _____ attain to thine eternal joy; through Jesus Christ, the author and perfecter

177

of our faith, who liveth and reigneth with thee and the Holy Spirit, one God, for ever and ever. Amen.

O God, who has brought us near to an innumerable company of angels and to the spirits of just men and women made perfect: Grant us during our earthly pilgrimage to abide in their fellowship, and in our heavenly country to become partakers of their joy; through Jesus Christ our Lord, who liveth and reigneth with thee and the Holy Spirit, one God, now and for ever. Amen.

O Almighty God, who by thy Holy Spirit has made us one with thy saints in heaven and on earth: Grant that in our earthly pilgrimage we may ever be supported by this fellowship of love and prayer, and may know ourselves to be surrounded by their witness to thy power and mercy. We ask this for the sake of Jesus Christ, in whom all our intercessions are acceptable through the Spirit, and who liveth and reigneth for ever and ever. Amen.

Lighting Vigil Candles

CANDLE LIGHTING, ANOTHER ANCIENT PRACTICE, IS A WAY of prayer. Long after our attention has moved on to other things, a lit votive candle symbolizes the intention of our love for God in Christ and the presence of our request before heaven. *Votive* comes from the Latin word *votum*, meaning vow, but *vigil*—a much better word for this practice—means watchfulness.

Candles are often set aside in the front or back of churches for this purpose. I will sometimes light one of these at my home parish, either before the service begins or immediately after taking Communion, as a prayer to my grandmother or as a petition for a needy friend.

Votive or vigil candles are usually considered symbols of Christ, the Light in the darkness, but they also can be powerful symbols of our own desire to be imitators of Christ, the true Light. When used in prayer, a candle can also show our persistence and continual desire to be with God, to listen for God's will, and to seek the intercession of one of the saints. I often use a candle in this spirit when I am reading or praying in the early morning and I am the only person awake in the house.

Many Christians from all denominations have small spaces called home altars where vigil candles are often kept and used for prayer. Like the psalmist, we may say, "Let my prayer be counted as incense before you, and the lifting up of my hands as an evening sacrifice" (Psalm 141:2).

February 2 is known as Candlemas on the Roman Catholic calendar. This feast celebrates the presentation of Jesus in the temple in Jerusalem. On Candlemas, candles traditionally receive a special blessing as we remember old Simeon's prophetic words upon seeing the child Jesus, whom he called "a light for revelation to the Gentiles and for glory to your people Israel" (Luke 2:32).

Before you get started, you should offer a blessing over your candles, sanctifying them for this purpose.

God of light, light to the nations,
light that reaches into all darkness,
use these candles to illuminate us.
May the light of our prayers always be with You,
quietly in Your holy presence,
and may we always be
reflected in Your true Light.
Amen.

Jesus said

"I have come into the world, so that whoever believes in me may not remain in darkness."

lighting a candle is a prayer

When we have gone it stays alight, kindling
in the hearts and minds of others
the prayers we have already offered;
for the sad - the sick - the suffering -
for the peace of the world -
and prayers for thankfulness too.

lighting a candle is a parable

Giving light to others, it burns itself out.
Christ gave himself for others -
he calls us to give ourselves.

lighting a candle is a symbol

of love and hope - of light and warmth -
our world needs them all.

PART FOUR

Reality and Practice

THE HOLY FATHERS WERE MAKING predictions about the last generation. They said, "What have we ourselves done?" One of them, the great Abba Ischyrion replied, "We ourselves have fulfilled the commandments of God." The others replied, "And those who come after us, what will they do?" He said, "They will struggle to achieve half our works." They said, "And to those who come after them, what will happen?" He said, "The people of that generation will not accomplish any works at all and temptation will come upon them; and those who will be approved in that day will be greater than either us or our fathers."

—The Sayings of the Desert Fathers[1]

Spiritual Imitation and
Hidden Saints

Be imitators of me, as I am of Christ.
—St. Paul, 1 Corinthians 11.1

I N *CHRIST RECRUCIFIED*, THE TWENTIETH-CENTURY
Greek novelist Nikos Kazantzakis portrays a small village
enacting a Passion play. The local Orthodox priest and
other village notables assign the various parts in the play to
people in the village who seem to fit the characters (St. Peter, St.
John, Christ, the Virgin Mary, Judas Iscariot, and so on), both in
physical appearance and in spirit or temperament. Each person
has one year to prepare for his or her part in the play, and the
play itself is of the utmost importance to the members of this
isolated, insular village. In the following passage, the priest
instructs the local proprietor of a café as to his role:

> You, Kostandis, are the man we have chosen to be James,
> the austere disciple of Christ. A heavy burden, a divine
> burden; bear it with dignity, do you hear? Do not dishonor
> the Apostle. From today you must become a new man,
> Kostandis. You are good, but you must become better.

More honest, more affable. Come to church more often. Put less barley in the coffee. Stop cutting the slabs of Turkish delight in two and selling the halves as wholes. Above all, take care not to beat your wife, because from today you are not only Kostandis, but also, and above all, James the Apostle. You understand? Do you?[1]

We have, in many ways, come full circle. In the preface to this book I confessed that I feel somewhat like Cervantes's Don Quixote in writing this study of saints and sainthood. It is foolish, isn't it, to think that reading and writing about saints will really satisfy a desire to drink deeply in the Spirit, as they have done?

Perhaps, but it can begin there, and it can be nurtured by reading, a step of imitation. Paul Elie, in his study of four twentieth-century Catholic writers (Flannery O'Connor, Thomas Merton, Dorothy Day, and Walker Percy), two of whom have many supporters for their causes for sainthood today (Day and Merton), says of them: "Emboldened by books, they set out to have for themselves the experiences they had read about, measuring their lives against the books that had struck them the most powerfully."[2] The lives of the martyrs and saints—from all eras—have always inspired readers to greater godliness, even through imitation.

Teachings of the saints also present us with valuable advice on how to live a life worthy of the title saint. St. Francis de Sales once quipped that the *Spiritual Exercises* of Ignatius of Loyola had probably made as many saints (of those who followed its precepts) as it had letters. And Sales's own *Introduction to the Devout Life* is designed as a handbook for sainthood. It details how to approach God through the life of the church and through prayer, how to avoid and overcome common temptations to sin, and the sixteen most important virtues.

Thomas à Kempis's *Imitation of Christ* has also influenced many. The most popular devotional book in history, it was a favorite also of Francis de Sales, and millions of others. Many other classics—which were classics long before the explosion of spirituality publishing in the late twentieth century—include Alfonso Rodriguez's *Christian Perfection* (1609), Walter

Hilton's *Ladder of Perfection* (1494), and, in the Eastern churches, the *Philokalia* (writings from the fourth to the fifteenth centuries, first published together in 1782).

Gregory the Great, medieval pope, liturgical reformer ("Gregorian" chant is named for him), and author of the influential *Life of St. Benedict,* wrote, "There are some who are moved to the love of God by examples of virtue, and others are more moved by sermons and doctrine." The early lives of the saints were intended for this purpose: to tell the stories of virtue and love of God so that the reader might be moved to earnestly try and do the same. For most of us, they speak louder than sermons and doctrine.

Thérèse of Lisieux, conscious of imitating sainthood from early childhood, once commented that the first word she was able to read without assistance from her parents was *heaven.* She was the youngest of five girls, each of whom entered a Carmelite convent. Practicing contemplative prayer for hours a day, she was intensely aiming at sainthood even before puberty. As an adolescent, she protested the convent's decision not to admit her at such a young age. Thérèse's father even traveled with her to Rome in the hope of petitioning the pope himself. While a nun, she kept track of the daily "sacrifices" she made for others and for God, as well as her "acts of love." Of the latter, Thérèse once recorded 2,773 in one three-month period.[3] At the end of her short life, Thérèse thought it ironic that she was dying at age twenty-four, as that would be the age at which she would be permitted to become a priest were she a man.

It sounds contrived, doesn't it, to aim so intently for sainthood? But Thérèse of the Child Jesus, as she was also known, provides the first true key toward an understanding of spiritual imitation. Lovely and childlike, fiercely intelligent and devoted, Thérèse was our first truly modern saint: a woman who shows us the way to holiness in our day. Near the end of her life, she recorded her experiences in a memoir that has since become one of the most popular spiritual books in history, *The Story of a Soul.* She describes how she wanted to become a true saint but failed to succeed at the public "face" of it all: the ascetical practice, gloomy face, and extraordinary behaviors. "The world of souls is the garden of Jesus," she wrote. We are all called to be saints—some to be like great lilies, others like daisies or violets. Becoming the saint that God intends us to become "consists in doing His will, in being that which He wants us to be."[4] Finding this identity that is ours in Christ is our perfection, our holiness, our sainthood.

St. Teresa of Avila is another successful example of spiritual imitation and self-conscious saintliness. She debunks any theories that all saints are born and not made. When Teresa was forced to write her autobiography, chronicling her childhood, her early sins and failures, and her visions and religious experiences, she told the truth. Her stories of a childhood filled with the wonder of the saints, and of being a child who wanted nothing more than to be one of them, ring true.

Like many children raised in devout Christian homes, Teresa was taught as a child that life on earth was a fleeting testing ground that would determine where we would go in the afterlife. She also learned of the martyrs of the church—Lucia and Catherine and the witness of hundreds of others throughout the churches of Avila—how they suffered for Christ and met their reward immediately after.

A precocious young girl, Teresa convinced her older brother, Rodrigo—she was seven; he was eleven—to sneak from the house one morning and wander beyond the immense city walls of Avila in search of infidels who might indulge their desire to be martyred for God as were the saints before them. The two of them used to read the lives of the saints together, and they were determined to be like them. Teresa writes that "we agreed to go off to the land of the Moors and beg them, out of love of God, to cut off our heads there. . . . Having parents seemed to us the greatest obstacle." The two siblings, of course, did not succeed in their plan, but soon afterward they desired to become hermits for God instead. In the family garden, Teresa and Rodrigo built small hermitages of stones and pretended to live there, praying fervently.[5] Years later, Teresa hadn't lost her desire to imitate saintliness with her brother. She wrote to him from the convent: "I send you this hair shirt. . . . It can be worn on any part of the body and put on in any way so long as it feels uncomfortable. . . . It makes me laugh to think how you send me sweets and presents and money, and I send you hair shirts."[6]

Chapter five discussed the making of saints by the Catholic church today, but we should also consider the making of our own sainthood. We need to learn to become more fully who we already are. There is nothing wrong with spiritual imitation. What is the ultimate reason for examining the lives of the saints if not, at least in part, to emulate them and somehow bring their virtue and goodness into our lives? The Torah says, "[B]e holy, for I the LORD your God am holy" (Leviticus 19:2). We can try that; God knows, many a Christian has felt alone trying to do so in the past.

Jesus added to Torah teaching by instructing us to seek the kingdom of God and do the will of the Father, which is ultimately different from seeking to be holy in tiny respects through adherence to the law. When we seek to be a part of God's kingdom—here on earth, not later in heaven—"these things will be given to you as well," Jesus said (Luke 12:31). Being a member of the kingdom of God is not effortless, but it also is not something that is earned. Ultimately, it falls somewhere in between and involves the will, a spirit tuned to God, and a desire for righteousness. Devotions and practices are tools to assist you. You may need prayers, candles, rosaries, and I may need some fasting and hair shirts. Becoming who we are is not like turning on a faucet or taking a shower. It requires our full attention and the help of one another—other saints.

"You are not far from the kingdom of God," Jesus says when we understand that the two greatest commandments are to love God and love our neighbor (Mark 12:34). So it would seem that righteousness is within our grasp. We not only follow the examples of those who have gone before us, but we also ask for help. The extravagance of the saints' lives, however, quickly convinces us that righteousness is not attainable. When we compare our efforts against their remarkable examples, we suffer by comparison. It is like applying for a good job and competing against a hundred other applicants; our credentials and experience are bound to look less impressive by comparison.

What we don't realize is that there are thousands of "secret" saints who have come and gone—those who aren't heroes on a large scale but may have lived nearly anonymous lives dedicated to God in quiet humility. They are not written up in books. Think

187

of the people in your life who may fit this category. For me, my grandmother comes immediately to mind. Clelia Bosette was born into an Italian-Catholic immigrant family. Her mother's parents had come to this country from Boretto, Italy, at about the time that her mother was born. It was the 1890s in the Great Plains of Kansas, and in order to better assimilate, the family shed its Catholicism and became nominally Protestant; the family also changed the spelling of its last name from Bosette to Bosetti, thinking it would further disguise the Italian. Faith had little influence in my grandmother's life until she was a young woman and both she and my grandfather had a conversion experience. They were "born again," and while my grandfather spent the next several decades preaching and teaching, my grandmother was always behind the scenes doing her own teaching (for women only, because women were only allowed to teach women in their tradition) and caring daily for the elderly and the forgotten in nursing homes. Her energy and example were extraordinary; she became my Mother Teresa. Also important for me were my grandmother's prayers. Every morning she prayed for me. Always wanting to know what I was doing, what I dreamed about, and knowing herself what was good for me and what God would want for my life, she prayed. What if, I have always wondered, my grandmother's prayers were heard more clearly by God than the prayers of the "greatest" of saints? Who is to say that heaven is more interested in one saint than another?

If you dislike the visibility of saintliness, consider its hidden-ness. Catholic novelist Flannery O'Connor, for instance, never wrote a story about a conscious saint; hers are not stories where you find any sanctity. Instead, she creates pictures of everyday people, usually those on the lower ends of social and economic ladders, who are somehow both weird and attractive at the same time. Isn't that almost what it means to be a saint? These characters show within themselves the tension between being both drawn to and revolted by the desire to be righteous. This tension shows our humanity, just as our sainthood is fully human. We all bear the image of Christ inside of us, on our faces, and in who we are to be.

Practices

Marek Czarnecki

AREK CZARNECKI HAS BEEN A WRITER OF
icons since 1991. He has been commissioned by
universities, parishes, and individuals, and his
work has been profiled in the *Hartford Courant* and *St. Anthony
Messenger* magazine. His studio, Seraphic Restorations, is
located in Avon, Connecticut.

> I know it is possible, but it is difficult for me to understand
> Christ and his gospel without the example of the saints.
> Honestly. So much of the gospel is written in the impera-
> tive tense. "Go forth" or "Teach all nations" or "Blessed
> are you when they persecute you for my sake." Here are a
> few more that come to mind: "Do unto others as you
> would have them do unto you," "Forgive seventy times
> seven times," and "Take up your cross and follow me." In
> the imperative, life is abstract, ideal, and philosophical.

189

In the present tense, it is active and concrete. Among a million reasons, I love the saints because they take Christianity out of the realm of pure, beautiful ideas and existentially live inside them. And succeed. It's not always comfortable or pretty, but they show the sum of what happens when someone becomes the variable, or unknown sum, in Christ's own ideal and divinely formulated equations.

As an iconographer, my day-to-day job is to realize the images of the saints in works of art, according to a traditional pictorial language that stretches back in time to the art in the catacombs. We prefer to say that we "write icons" instead of painting them, because they are not just pictures but living texts, ones that are in perfect harmony with the written text of the gospel. There are hundreds of thousands of recognized saints, and also the multitude "known only to God." As part of my personal spiritual practice, every day I read my *Butler's Lives of the Saints,* sometimes four or five for any given day; they are all dizzyingly different. Like musicians trying to interpret the same piece of music, the saints had the same objective in mind: how can I imitate Jesus, or, as we say in iconography, be an "image bearer of Christ"? Paradoxically, how can there be so many different manifestations of the same path? How is it possible to explain this multiplicity and diversity when, before the throne of God, they are all enthroned on the same bench in front of the same beautiful vision? Can you imagine Dorothy Day sitting next to Pope Pius the IX?

Christ is so great, so infinite, that it is humanly impossible to take him all in, completely, especially with the limitations of our backgrounds, culture, bodies, and personalities. So it is amazing to see what happens when that infinite potential by consent, hard existential work, and the gifts of grace are squeezed into the human heart, and not only to read about it, but also to watch our friends and neighbors arrive at the fullness of its expression in tangible results. We can digest and realize only a small amount of that divine potential that was in Christ, but even a small fraction of infinity is still infinite. All together, the communion of saints creates a panoramic encyclopedia of human experience, and, as St. Teresa of Avila said, "It is possible to know God through all things."

Many of my friends (who are artists as well as other iconographers and priests) laugh at me for a horrible lapse I have in taste. I love the factory-made plaster statuary that fills Catholic churches, with their sentimental and inaccurate likenesses. I restore them for churches and people's home shrines, and my home is a dense forest of orphaned statues (a friend called me "Pope Gepetto" when she saw my "saint hospital"). I love them, not because they set an aesthetic standard but because of their warmth and ability to put a human face on the Christian experience, and their accessibility to all people. As St. Paul says, "we are surrounded by a mighty cloud of witnesses," and here they are. Here are their faces, standing in our churches, on our stained-glass windows, or on a big white doily on my grandfather's bureau. Like many Catholics, I was heartbroken in the 1970s when the Catholic church began modernizing and renovating its immigrant-founded sanctuaries, taking the saints off their pedestals, sealing them into their niches, or marginalizing them to the stairwells and storage closets.

I know that neither God nor the saints need icons of themselves, but we do. The image of a saint is an important tool for storytelling and commemoration and a place where their successes and sufferings can be seen and glorified. The icon is not just a picture but a window that connects us to the person it represents, and who is standing at the portal to encourage us that it is really possible to be a Christian. Each one expands the realm of possibility for success and a new feat in human experience. With iconoclasm (the destruction and suppression of the images of the saints), the saints' examples, stories, and living presence also are forgotten, as is the chance of us finding an individual way for ourselves.

I am especially thrilled when a church or a client brings me a forgotten or local saint from a nation's specific pantheon of holiness. Who was St. Oronzo of Lecce? St. Casimir of Lithuania? St. Peter Chanel? St. Trifomena? St. Stanislaus Kostka? And why was such a grand image of this person cast? And then mass-produced? You mean there are hundreds, or thousands, of copies of this image in the world? Why bother remembering them?

It is exciting when a parish commissions an icon of a newly recognized saint: St. Rafqa of Lebanon, Blessed Kateri Tekakwitha, or St. Faustina Kowalska. An art historian once asked me to explain the popularity of St. John Neupomuk in Mexican art, and all I could pragmatically say was "Because he answered peoples' prayers and helped them." I know this issue of the intercession of the saints will sound strange to many, but honestly, I find it a natural and easy-to-believe dogma. Our common and ecumenical understanding is that the grave does not separate us from anything or anyone, because love cannot be destroyed.

The new hagiographies are refreshingly honest, emphasizing the spontaneous and existential as well as, at times, quite ugly sides of them. We see them as not very perfect people but ones who knew how to love despite serious and heavy shortcomings, and love in a way few people on earth ever can. They give us a new and realistic view of a normal life and what really makes a person Christian and holy. I loved reading a passage from the canonization procedure of St. Frances Cabrini, who died in the twentieth century. One of her friends said: "She was a saint? I didn't know that, and neither did she." She worked tirelessly for the dignity and respect of Italian immigrants, founding hospitals and orphanages, yet was merciless and cruel to pregnant, unwed girls (St. Frances Cabrini, forgive me for writing about your shortcomings).

I read with trashy interest a critical article about Mother Teresa demanding parking privileges when visiting New York City (only if you've lived in New York City and owned a car can you understand the magnitude of indulgence she was requesting). And later when I watched her help someone die, I thought, let her have the parking space. In sadness, shame, and arrogance, I knew I would never rise to the beauty of that one example, which I knew for her was only one of thousands of people she had helped pass with love and dignity, and for her was a typical day.

I am relieved to be able to read in the new hagiographies less of an emphasis on reconciling the person to the format of propaganda and more on letting the saint speak for him- or herself. Over the sink, I have a photograph of St. Thérèse of Lisieux washing her laundry in the convent pool. In her handwriting beneath the photo is a caption that says, *À l'extase je préfère la monotonie du sacrifice* ("To ecstasy, I prefer the monotony of sacrifice"). We can really see the Holy Spirit working in the saints, as well as their natural charisms, for ourselves.

It is dangerous to put words in the mouths of the saints, to not let them plainly speak for themselves, whether we agree or disagree with them. This was a dilemma for me when I was commissioned to write the icon of St. Maria Goretti, a twelve-year-old girl who died while defending herself against a rapist and on her deathbed not only forgave him but prayed for his salvation. Was it right to set out her example in an icon? The reality of the saints is that their experiences can be so outside the box of previous human experience. The priest who asked me to write her icon gave me a wealth of material to read about her, and what I felt most was the authority of her own decision, and I was in no position to edit or change it. I was discussing this saint and her image with my iconography teacher, and she said, "See? We have no idea who is strong until we are tested." No one had the right to force himself on Maria, to take her body, or to destroy her soul. And no human court would have denied her the right of justice or revenge, which she not only declined but inverted. I still am pondering the issues her life and death raise, and I am troubled and awed by her.

Another reason why we should not manipulate the saints to suit our own interpretations is that one of their most vital jobs is to rebuke the complacency and abuses of the Christian church by their example, and how astonished the church itself is at their extraordinary conscience. I remember reading a prayer in honor of St. Francis that started "Lord, when the world had grown cold and forgotten you, you sent your servant Francis." So it is no surprise to read about St. Catherine of Siena's struggles with both popes and antipopes in the years of schism. Or that St. John of the Cross was put in prison by the Inquisition, or that St. Elizabeth of Hungary suffered from a cruel and sadistic confessor. We are still trying to sort out figures like Savanarola, and it took hundreds of years for us to recognize Joan of Arc as St. Joan and not as a lunatic and patriotic witch. As Dorothy Day said, "The church is the cross on which Christ is crucified" (which is probably why her canonization is going so slowly), and as our Lord said, "If they persecuted me, they will persecute you also."

I have an embarrassing confession to make, one that is especially painful in front of my friends in the Reformed churches, and it is that I have never read the Bible from cover to cover (slowly, I am making amends for this lapse). But I understand its message from the example of the saints, and, obliquely, I have read it through their lives.

CHAPTER

12

Ten Rough Guidelines for
Living as a Saint Today

AFTER READING THE LIVES OF HUNDREDS OF saints who have lived down through the centuries, it is possible to pinpoint at least ten frequently repeated features in the lives of those who have been recognized as saints. These might be ten steps for those striving to live as a saint today. Each is presented here in the contemporary language of spiritual practice, highlighting how it might be possible to use these steps in daily life today. They are in no particular order.

1. Saints use primitive means of helping themselves toward conversion (a lifelong process, beyond salvation). Chief among these primitive methods are journeys—usually by foot or some other slow process—that serve as penance or simply as a time for solitude.

2. Saints have private relationships with God. Their closet expressions—quiet, uncomplicated, and alone with God—become the foundation for the saintly things they do later.

3. Saints have developed heightened sensitivities to and perceptions of the thoughts, desires, and needs of those around them. Often regarded as miraculous, this ability is known, in theological language, as discernment.

4. Saints help others toward conversion with an easy understanding of sin, as well as release from sin.

5. Saints are lovers of life, not just heaven. Even the martyrs, who willingly give up their lives, know how great a sacrifice that is. Just as a saint loves God, creator of all things, a saint also loves the creation and works to change or remove those human institutions that stand in the way of others' love of life.

6. Saints are very self-aware; they question themselves—their motives, actions, feelings—with great honesty.

7. Saints see the holy throughout the phenomena of the natural world. They see connections between people and animals, and between people and people, that seem obvious to them and few others. They are good mediators, reconcilers, healers. These skills are so uncommon in the world that they seem miraculous when we experience them.

8. Saints serve God and humanity from the underside. Many a saint has had aristocratic beginnings, to be sure, but it is difficult to remember one who did not actually become a saint by leaving that behind.

9. Saints are able to pay attention, sit still for a long time, and do the same thing over and over again. They do not seek much entertainment but, rather, become skilled at things.

10. Saints listen more than they talk or ask questions.

And here are two bonus guidelines:

1. Saints are often misunderstood. They often have trouble at home and at school and are misunderstood by parents,

siblings, and contemporaries. This trend imitates the remarkably dismissive comments made at times by Jesus to his own mother but also mirrors the divine purpose attached to many of the disputes known in every home with teenagers. Imagine Catherine of Siena's mother, for instance— a mother to twenty-five—when Catherine, the youngest, sheared her long, blond hair so as to spend less time accepting suitors and more time in prayer and seclusion.

2. Saints practice resurrection: they are continually working to put aside any things or relationships or pursuits that are not eternal and to help others along the path to do the same.

Practices

Rev. Mary E. Haddad

REV. MARY E. HADDAD IS ASSOCIATE RECTOR OF St. Bartholomew's (Episcopal) Church in New York, New York. She is a graduate of the General Theological Seminary and is recognized for her inspiring teaching ministries. Texts of her sermons and information about the innovative work of St. Bart's, located in midtown Manhattan, can be found at www.stbarts.org.

The calendar of the Episcopal church makes it almost impossible not to interact with the saints. Several years ago, I was the resident verger of All Saints Episcopal Church in Beverly Hills, California, and a frequent lay preacher. I especially remember preparing to preach for the feast day of St. Francis of Assisi, because living at the church in the heart of Beverly Hills provided a perfect context for musing about his life. As I went about my business, running errands and moving around town, I jostled alongside the rich and famous, and I walked my dog in the park along Santa Monica Boulevard among the homeless. The medieval Italian story of St. Francis had a parallel right before my eyes.

Pietro Bernadone of Assisi was the Giorgio Armani of his day, and he loved weaving fabulous clothes. His son Francis Bernadone loved wearing them, until his conversion, when he gave away his father's bolts of clothing and ran through the town naked, shifting the center of his life from the shop on Rodeo Drive, as it were, to the park across the street. For me, Francis ceased to be the quaint saint presiding over birdbaths in beautiful gardens and became more like a stinking, crazy homeless person along Santa Monica Boulevard, talking to a tree. I also came to see that his father, Pietro, as the owner of an upscale clothing boutique, would have been more likely to be welcomed as a dinner guest or parishioner at our church than his son would. Once I came to see Francis this way, I became forever disabused of his romanticized reputation, and I was awakened to the hypocritical tendencies we show toward "the least of these" who are always in our midst.

One spiritual discipline I have adopted that I attribute to my relationship with St. Francis is frequently purging my apartment and office of superfluous material things. I'll give things away rather than keep them in storage, and I continually try to live without accumulating unnecessary belongings.

One other quick reflection: I always request to preach on the anniversary of my priestly ordination, which falls on the feast day of St. Thomas Aquinas (January 28). This gives me an opportunity to interact with his writings once a year. In addition, my birthday (October 23) falls on the feast day of St. James of Jerusalem, the brother of our Lord. I happen to have a brother who was born on Christmas Eve. It is good fun to share with a congregation that I know exactly how James of Jerusalem must have felt, because I too have a brother who was born on Christmas Eve!

Becoming Saints

J ESUS SETS THE STANDARD OF HOLINESS SO HIGH IN
the Sermon on the Mount that none of us can seemingly
reach it. Do the saints we honor reach this high?

When Jesus saw the crowds, he went up the mountain; and
after he sat down, his disciples came to him. Then he began
to speak, and taught them, saying:

"Blessed are the poor in spirit, for theirs is the kingdom
of heaven.

"Blessed are those who mourn, for they will be comforted.

"Blessed are the meek, for they will inherit the earth.

"Blessed are those who hunger and thirst for righteousness,
for they will be filled.

"Blessed are the merciful, for they will receive mercy.

"Blessed are the pure in heart, for they will see God.

"Blessed are the peacemakers, for they will be called
children of God.

"Blessed are those who are persecuted for righteousness'
sake, for theirs is the kingdom of heaven.

"Blessed are you when people revile you and persecute you and utter all kinds of evil against you falsely on my account. Rejoice and be glad, for your reward is great in heaven, for in the same way they persecuted the prophets who were before you." (Matthew 5:1–12)

There is no doubt that great saints have used Jesus' teaching as a list of what to do, what not to do, and who to try to become. Many have succeeded to an extraordinary degree of faithfulness.

In the sermon, Jesus continues:

"You are the salt of the earth; but if salt has lost its taste, how can its saltiness be restored? It is no longer good for anything, but is thrown out and trampled under foot.

"You are the light of the world. A city built on a hill cannot be hid. No one after lighting a lamp puts it under the bushel basket, but on the lampstand, and it gives light to all in the house. In the same way, let your light shine before others, so that they may see your good works and give glory to your Father in heaven." (Matthew 5:13–16)

Jesus concludes this portion of his teaching with the sentence that has been bemoaned by Christians for millennia: "Be perfect, therefore, as your heavenly Father is perfect" (Matthew 5:48). How is that at all possible?

My friend Professor Ron Miller of Lake Forest College in Illinois offers a helpful explanation of how we might understand these teachings of Jesus—and it goes a long way toward explaining how we all might really become the saints we are intended to become. Miller retranslates Matthew 5:48 this way: "You should grow to your fullness, becoming whole and holy, like your heavenly Parent." And he offers this short explanation:

I used to fear the word "perfect," seeing in it an impossible ideal. But when I first read this passage in German, I noticed that the word was *vollkommen*, a clear cognate to the English phrase "to come full." We are to come full, like the rose in its fullness or the full moon, like the full-faced smile of a baby or the full fruit ripened on the vine. God is the fullness of existence, and we are called to be fully all that we have the capacity to be. [Jesus'] call is to a full and abundant life.[1]

Above all else, saints have discovered what, for them, is the true likeness of God in their lives. They do not suffer, as the rest of us do, from wandering in what Sts. Augustine and Bernard of Clairvaux called "the Land of Unlikeness." Each of us at one time had a likeness that was only like unto our Creator, but few of us in maturity have been able to retain it. Instead, we more often are found somewhat lost, unlike ourselves as we once were.

To become a saint is not to become otherworldly as much as to become fully human. Some hagiographers did not understand this, no doubt, but Christ taught it. He showed us how to be fully human and divine all at the same time. He showed us the way to the most fulfilling, abundant life. Guibert of Nogent, one of the theologians of the Middle Ages who helped articulate the church's reasons for the veneration of saints' relics, once said, "Anything that is connected with the Divine is in itself Divine, and nothing is more closely connected with the Divine than God's saints who are of one body with him." Yes! In a very real sense—so real, in fact, that it is not unreasonable to find holiness in the very stuff of it—the saints of God share in Christ's body.

St. Ambrose once said, after the discovery of the relics of Sts. Gervasius and Protasius, "Our eyes have opened to behold God's glory, which is seen in the passion of the martyrs and present in the working of their lives." Similarly, Thornton Wilder says at the end of *Our Town* that the "eternal part of us" can only come through when we make room in our lives for God's gracious filling and become as fully human as we are already made spiritual by God.

The communion of saints is all around us, all the time. They are listening, available, right before us. We, too, are saints when we are alive in Christ. It is the extraordinariness of this realization that caused pilgrims to gather up the blood from Thomas à Becket's crushed skull as he lay dying on the cold floor of Canterbury Cathedral. That's the weirdness of the saints that so fascinates us. But the same realization that saints' bodies are one with Christ's body shows us how to make sense of sainthood today, and how to take our own potential as saints more seriously.

SPIRITUALITY IS INCIDENTAL

The pursuit of saintliness can be an honest and earnest endeavor, but it is ultimately misguided. You might diligently follow a list like the one in chapter twelve—ten guidelines for becoming a saint, for instance—but doing those things will not get you there in and of itself. I don't even think that becoming a saint is the same as practicing spirituality. Practicing spirituality is part of saintliness, to be sure, but not the crux of it.

We make a mistake when we simply interpret the saints' lives as exemplars of an ideal spiritual life. Certainly saints are more focused on what is spiritual, lasting, and eternal than on that which is natural or bound to pass away. Most of our lives differ from the lives of the saints in this important regard, but when we say that the saints are spiritual we should understand that there are two things that spirituality is not. First, spirituality is not a permanent condition; it is not something that you enter into like a bath, and it is also not an acquired or temporary condition, like hunger or its opposite, satiety. Second—even though it sounds incorrect to say so—spirituality is not meant to be the goal of our lives. We spend a lot of time trying to be spiritual, in all that that means, and most of it is good, but God does not ask us to be spiritual; God asks us to become like Christ, to become Christ in our own unique way, which as Thomas Merton explains means to become ourselves.

Listen in as Merton introduces this idea to young men at the Abbey of Gethsemani in Kentucky who are preparing to become monks:

> There is only one thing for anybody to become in life. There's no point in becoming spiritual. It's a waste of time—the whole thing, trying to make yourself spiritual. You're not; it's a waste of time. What you came here for, what you came anywhere for, is to become yourself, to discover your complete identity, to be you! But the catch to that, of course, is that our full identity as monks and as Christians

is Christ. It is Christ in each one of us. . . . I've got to become me in such a way that I am the Christ that can only be Christ in me. There is a Louie-Christ which must be brought into existence and hasn't matured yet; it has a long way to go![2]

Sainthood is utterly and completely incarnational. Sainthood is the marriage of God and the individual man or woman, flesh and spirit, heavenly and earthly, transcendent and imminent, in a kind of perfection that is available and possible today. It is ordinary in its simplicity but miraculous and extraordinary at the same time. It happened to you before you were born—God made it possible in Christ—and now you must know it and grow into it. If you allow God to be as close to you as to enflesh you, being a saint, living your vocation, will become natural.

There is a tradition in Judaism that if you are about to plant a tree and you hear that the Messiah has come, you should go ahead and plant your tree before you go out to meet him. The point of the teaching is this: the people of God bring about the kingdom of God. Do what you do to bring about the kingdom. In that is your sainthood.

Make Your Own Novena

A FTER CHRIST'S ASCENSION INTO HEAVEN FROM Mount Olivet, the disciples did not know what to do. They were confused, afraid, and uncertain. For nine days, the eleven disciples, Mary the Mother of Jesus, and possibly Mary Magdalene stayed together in a house in Jerusalem waiting on God and discussing what had happened. This is where we find the first reference to "the upper room" as a place of prayerful discernment; these prayerful disciples were meeting in the upper room in the house where they were staying.

Jesus asked them to wait in Jerusalem and to wait on the Lord in prayer, according to Acts 1:4: "While staying with them [during the forty days between the Resurrection and the Ascension], [Jesus] ordered them not to leave Jerusalem, but to wait there for the promise of the Father." We know that they were reading the Hebrew Scriptures together in that upper room,

207

as well as praying for God's will and direction. They also elected the twelfth apostle, a replacement for Judas.

Tradition has it that the disciples stayed together in prayer for nine days, seeking God's will and wisdom. Nine days after the Ascension—following this period of waiting on God—the Holy Spirit was poured out as celebrated in today's churches as the day of Pentecost.

The practice of "making"—or faithfully praying—novenas reaches back many centuries. A novena is a prayer that symbolizes the vigil of those nine days in seclusion. The word *novena* means nine, and novenas always have something to do with the number nine; they are often prayers that are prayed nine times a day for nine consecutive days.

Each novena is occasioned by a personal need or request, and the novena is prayed to either God the Father, the Son, or the Holy Spirit, Mary, or one of the saints. Novenas are common as a practice for people with specific, serious needs. There are books and pamphlets of novenas, for instance, to the patron saints of cancer patients (St. Peregrine; d. 1345), mothers (St. Anne, mother of the Virgin Mary), the emotionally troubled (St. Dymphna; seventh century), and arthritis sufferers (St. Alphonsus Liguori; d. 1787). Unfortunately, the use of novena prayers in recent times has turned from a waiting on the Lord to a more banal sort of petitionary prayer, or the simple asking of favors. A novena is not supposed to be a way of tapping into the magic of a saint, as devotions to patron saints sometimes do, but instead can be a way of asking a particular saint to help guide us in creating a heart or spirit like theirs in us as well.

I make novenas to saints in the spirit of simple faithfulness, making the same request again and again each day for nine days. I will often do this when I have concerns or worries that are weighing heavily on my mind. I find that it is often easier to listen for answers to prayer and guidance as a result of prayer when the time frame is extended to nine full days. Occasionally, I extend my vigil for nine weeks, returning to a saint, or to Mary, in prayer each morning upon waking up and each evening before getting into bed.

Acknowledgments
and Permissions

I OWE MANY THANKS TO ANNE MCCORMICK AND THE Merton Legacy Trust for their permission to quote from a talk given by Thomas Merton at the Abbey of Gethsemani in Kentucky on William Faulkner's "The Bear." I am also grateful to many teachers and friends who shared with me their own relationships and spiritual practices with saints and are quoted throughout the book: Abbot M. Basil Pennington, O.C.S.O.; Mitch Finley; Sr. Rosemarie Greco, D.W.; Fr. Murray Bodo, O.F.M.; Br. Wayne Teasdale; Marek Czarnecki; and Rev. Mary E. Haddad. Thank you also to Brother Richard, Brother John, Brother Elias, and all of the monks at Weston Priory in Weston, Vermont, who have been supportive of my spiritual life and work. Thanks, also, to Father Matt at Our Lady of the Holy Spirit, Conyers, Georgia; our long conversations have taught me much. But most of all, I am endebted to my wife, Danelle, who teaches me more about saintliness than one could ever learn from history or books.

✦ ✦ ✦

All English translations from the Bible are from the New Revised Standard Version. Most of the small illustrations are taken from the scarce and lovely old book *Lives and Legends of the Great Hermits and Fathers of the Church, with Other Contemporary Saints,* by Mrs. Arthur Bell (London: George Bell & Sons, 1902). The photographs on pages 42, 80, 83, 231, and 235 were taken by the author in New York, New York; Trappist, Kentucky; and London, England, in 2004.

Shared Saints and Feasts Between Roman Catholic, Orthodox, and Anglican (Episcopal) Churches

THE FOLLOWING SAINTS ARE CELEBRATED IN EACH OF the three oldest traditions within Christianity. While this is not an exhaustive list, it is a place for the ecumenically inclined to share an appreciation for saints that reaches across cultures and denominational differences. I have deliberately excluded the New Testament apostles and have focused only on saints from later centuries. Unfortunately, saints from beyond the tenth century CE are not shared between the Eastern churches and the Roman Catholic church. Each saint listed below, however, is the equivalent of a patron saint of ecumenism.

The feast day listed is the day observed in the Roman Catholic church. (Dates in the Eastern churches often differ.)

Antony of Egypt	January 17
Athanasius	May 2
Basil the Great	January 2

Clement of Rome	November 23
Cyprian of Carthage	September 16
Cyril of Jerusalem	March 18
Cyril and Methodius (brothers)	February 14
Ephrem of Syria	June 9
Gregory Nazianzen	January 2
Helena	August 18
The Holy Innocents	December 28
Irenaeus	June 28
John Chrysostom	September 13
John of Damascus	December 4
Lawrence of Rome	August 10
Leo the Great	November 10
Nicholas of Myra	December 6
Polycarp	February 23

NOTES

INTRODUCTION

1. Sr. Joan Chittister, in conversation with the author and others, Smith College, Northampton, MA, October 19, 2003.
2. Daniel J. Wakin, obituary of James O'Gara, *New York Times,* November 1, 2003.
3. Roberto Pazzi, "Why the Next Pope Needs to Be Italian," *New York Times,* January 11, 2004.
4. Garry Wills, *Why I Am a Catholic* (Boston: Mariner Books/Houghton Mifflin, 2003), xi.
5. Richard P. McBrien, *Lives of the Saints: From Mary and St. Francis of Assisi to John XXIII and Mother Teresa* (New York: HarperCollins, 2003), 226.

Part 1

1. St. Anselm, *The Prayers and Meditations of Saint Anselm,* trans. Benedicta Ward, S.L.G. (New York: Penguin, 1973), 213-14.

CHAPTER 1

1. Julian Green, *Paris,* trans. J. A. Underwood (New York: Marion Boyars, 2001), 37.
2. Ibid., 91.
3. Scott Hahn, *The Lamb's Supper: The Mass as Heaven on Earth* (New York: Doubleday, 1999), 7.
4. Elizabeth A. Johnson, *Friends of God and Prophets: A Feminist Theological Reading of the Communion of Saints* (New York: Continuum, 2003), 2.

CHAPTER 2

1. Augustine of Hippo, *Sermons to the People: Advent, Christmas, New Year's, Epiphany,* trans. and ed. William Griffin (New York: Image Books/Doubleday, 2002), 6-7.

2. Jon Sobrino, quoted in Stephen Tierney, "In the Garden of San Romero," *Tablet,* August 28, 2004.

3. Tom Mueller, "Inside Job," *Atlantic Monthly,* October 2003, 142.

4. Peter Brown, *The Cult of the Saints: Its Rise and Function in Latin Christianity* (Chicago: University of Chicago Press, 1981), 119. The preceding insight about Gregory of Tours also comes from this passage in Brown's book.

5. Ibid., 3.

6. "Goings On About Town," *New Yorker,* April 19 and 26, 2004, 32.

CHAPTER 3

1. Nikos Kazantzakis, *Report to Greco,* trans. P. A. Bien (New York: Simon & Schuster, 1965), 77-78.

2. G. K. Chesterton, *Orthodoxy* (New York: Doubleday, 1936), 49.

3. Andrew Greeley, *The Catholic Imagination* (Berkeley: University of California Press, 2001), 5. Greeley is summarizing the work of Catholic theologian David Tracy.

4. R. Scott Appleby, "Unheavenly Days," *New York Times Book Review,* September 7, 2003, 12.

5. Mark S. Massa, S.J., *Anti-Catholicism in America: The Last Acceptable Prejudice* (New York: Crossroad Publishing, 2003), 52.

6. Andrew Greeley, *The Catholic Imagination* (Berkeley: University of California Press, 2001), 1.

7. Scott Hahn, *The Lamb's Supper: The Mass as Heaven on Earth* (New York: Doubleday, 1999), 42.

8. James Martin, S.J., "Contemporary Catholics on Traditional Devotions," *America,* March 3, 2003.

9. Alan Cowell, "The Selling of Blessed Mother Teresa," *New York Times,* October 19, 2003.

10. Kathryn Harrison, *Saint Thérèsa of Lisieux* (New York: Viking Press, 2003), 4.

CHAPTER 4

1. Paul Hetherington, trans., *The Painter's Manual of Dionysius of Fourna* (Torrance, California: Oakwood Publications, 1989), 61.
2. Richard P. McBrien, *Lives of the Saints: From Mary and St. Francis of Assisi to John XXIII and Mother Teresa* (New York: HarperCollins, 2003), 384.
3. Ibid., 123.
4. Quoted by Jim Forest, in Mother Maria Skobtsova, introduction to *Mother Maria Skobtsova: Essential Writings,* trans. Richard Pevear and Larissa Volokhonsky (Maryknoll, NY: Orbis Books, 2003), 20.
5. Mother Maria Skobtsova, *Mother Maria Skobtsova: Essential Writings,* trans. by Richard Pevear and Larissa Volokhonsky (Maryknoll, NY: Orbis Books, 2003), 47, 48-49.
6. Joseph Cardinal Bernardin. This talk, and many others, is available at http://archives.archchicago.org/default.htm, the Web site of the Archdiocese of Chicago's Joseph Cardinal Bernardin Archives & Records Center, Chicago, Illinois.
7. Hella Pick, "Cardinal Franz König," *Guardian,* March 16, 2004. Other information about Cardinal König is taken from Pick's obituary.

CHAPTER 5

1. Lesley Hazleton, *Mary: A Flesh-and-Blood Biography of the Virgin Mother* (New York: Bloomsbury, 2004), 1.
2. Evelyn Waugh's character, Cordelia, says of Lady Marchmain in *Brideshead Revisited:* "She was saintly but she wasn't a saint."

Part 2

1. Dorothy Day, *On Pilgrimage* (Grand Rapids, MI: Wm. B. Eerdmans Publishing, 1999), 75–92. Originally published in *The Catholic Worker* newspaper.

CHAPTER 6

1. Throughout this short section, I am indebted to Kenneth L. Woodward's *Making Saints: How the Catholic Church Determines Who Becomes a Saint, Who Doesn't, and Why* (New York: Simon and Schuster, 1990).

2. Venerable Bede, "Cuthbert's Letter on the Death of Bede," in *Ecclesiastical History of the English People,* eds. Bertram Colgrave and R. A. B. Mynors (Oxford: Clarendon Press, 1969), 585.

3. Kathryn Harrison, *Saint Thérèse of Lisieux* (New York: Viking Press, 2003), 3.

4. Kenneth L. Woodward, *Making Saints: How the Catholic Church Determines Who Becomes a Saint, Who Doesn't, and Why* (New York: Simon and Schuster, 1990), 313.

CHAPTER 7

1. Dante, *Purgatory,* trans. Dorothy L. Sayers (Baltimore: Penguin Books, 1960), 250, line 126.

2. Dante, *Purgatory,* trans. and ed. Anthony Esolen (New York: Modern Library, 2003), xv.

3. Eamon Duffy, *The Stripping of the Altars: Traditional Religion in England, 1400–1580* (New Haven: Yale University Press, 1992), 156.

4. Martin Luther, "Preface to Vol. 1 of His Latin Writings," in *Martin Luther's 95 Theses,* ed. Kurt Aland (St. Louis: Concordia, 1967), 25.

5. Ibid., 33.

6. Ibid., 35.

7. James Carroll, *Constantine's Sword: The Church and the Jews* (New York: Mariner Books, 2002), 559.

8. James Joyce, *A Portrait of the Artist as a Young Man* (New York: Penguin Books, 2003), 265.

9. Roland H. Bainton, *Here I Stand: A Life of Martin Luther* (New York: Meridian/Penguin Books, 1995), 120.

10. J. R. H. Moorman, *A History of the Church in England,* 3rd ed. (Harrisburg, PA: Morehouse Publishing, 1980), 208-9.

11. Friedrich Nietzsche, *The Gay Science,* trans. Walter Kaufmann (New York: Vintage Books, 1974), no. 27.

12. Kathryn Harrison, *Saint Thérèse of Lisieux* (New York: Viking Press, 2003), 56-57.

CHAPTER 8

1. Scott Hahn, *Lord, Have Mercy: The Healing Power of Confession* (New York: Doubleday, 2003), 53.

2. Scott Hahn, *Hail, Holy Queen: The Mother of God in the Word of God* (New York: Doubleday, 2001), 107.

3. Emile Mâle, *The Gothic Image: Religious Art in France of the Thirteenth Century*, trans. Dora Nussey (New York: Harper & Brothers, 1958), 280.

4. Jim Gallagher, *Padre Pio: A Holy Priest* (London: Catholic Truth Society, Publishers to the Holy See, 2002), 20.

5. Venerable Bede, *Ecclesiastical History of the English People*, ed. Bertram Colgrave and R. A. B. Mynors (Oxford: Clarendon Press, 1969), xxxvi.

6. Gerald of Wales, *The Journey through Wales and The Description of Wales*, trans. Lewis Thorpe (New York: Penguin Books, 1978), 83-84.

7. Adomnan of Iona, *Life of St. Columba*, trans. Richard Sharpe (New York: Penguin Books, 1995), 112. Tense has been changed from third to first person.

8. Tim Severin, *The Brendan Voyage* (New York: Modern Library, 2000), 15.

9. Umberto Eco, "James Bond," quoted in and trans. Alison Goddard Elliot, *Roads to Paradise: Reading the Lives of the Early Saints* (Hanover, NH: University Press of New England, 1987), 7-8.

10. Sarah Churchwell, "Lourdes in a Logging Town," review of *Our Lady of the Forest*, by David Guterson, *New York Times Literary Supplement,* November 21, 2003, 21.

11. I am indebted to Thomas Moore, author of *Care of the Soul,* for the seed of this point. In a public lecture at Harvard in November 1999, and in conversation with the author and others beforehand, he made the comment that the Greek gods and goddesses are like saints among us all the time. "It is a wonder that we don't see Achilles on the street," he said, which I have always found to be a provocative insight.

12. Simone Weil, *Letter to a Priest*, trans. A. F. Wills (New York: G. P. Putnam's Sons, 1954), 57.

13. Bridget of Sweden, trans. Elizabeth Spearing, quoted in *Medieval Writings on Female Spirituality,* ed. Elizabeth Spearing (New York: Penguin Books, 2002), 146-47.

14. Daniel Berrigan, quoted in Kenneth L. Woodward, *Making Saints: How the Catholic Church Determines Who Becomes a Saint, Who Doesn't, and Why* (New York: Simon & Schuster, 1990), 35.

Part 3

1. St. Thérèse of Lisieux, *The Autobiography of St. Thérèse of Lisieux: The Story of a Soul*, trans. John Beevers (New York: Image Books, 2001), 160.

CHAPTER 9

1. Simone Weil, *Letter to a Priest*, trans. A. F. Wills (New York: G. P. Putnam's Sons, 1954), 53.

2. Hilary Mantel, "Some Girls Want Out," review of four books about saints, *London Review of Books*, March 4, 2004, 15.

3. Teresa of Avila, *The Complete Works of St. Teresa of Avila*, trans. E. Allison Peers (London: Sheed & Ward, 1946), 192-93.

4. See the fascinating book *The Voices of Gemma Galgani: The Life and Afterlife of a Modern Saint*, by Rudolph Bell and Cristina Mazzoni (Chicago: University of Chicago Press, 2003) for more on this interesting modern saint.

5. Gerard Manley Hopkins, *Journals and Papers of Gerard Manley Hopkins*, ed. Humphry House and Graham Storey (New York: Oxford University Press, 1959), 195.

6. Fyodor Dostoyevsky, *The Idiot*, trans. Richard Pevear and Larissa Volokhonsky (New York: Alfred A. Knopf, 2002), 163-68.

7. This quote and the one preceding it are taken from letters written by Dostoyevsky in January 1868. Quoted in Richard Pevear, introduction to *The Idiot*, by Fyodor Dostoyevsky, trans. Richard Pevear and Larissa Volokhonsky (New York: Alfred A. Knopf, 2002), xv.

8. V. Sackville-West, *The Eagle and the Dove: A Study in Contrasts—St. Teresa of Avila, St. Thérèse of Lisieux* (London: Michael Joseph, Ltd., 1943), 177.

9. Louise Collis, *The Apprentice Saint* (London: Michael Joseph, Ltd., 1964), 22.

10. E. M. Cioran, *Tears and Saints*, trans. Ilinca Zarifopol-Johnston (Chicago: University of Chicago Press, 1995), 37.

11. Bridget Morris, ed., *St. Birgitta of Sweden* (Woodbridge, UK: Boydell, 1999), 54.

CHAPTER 10

1. Letter from Thérèse of Lisieux to her sister Celine, October 14, 1890, quoted in Thérèse of Lisieux, *Letters of St. Thérèse of Lisieux, Volume II 1890–1897*, trans. John Clarke, O.C.D. (Washington, DC: Institute of Carmelite Studies, 1988), 709.

2. Elizabeth Spearing, ed., *Medieval Writings on Female Spirituality* (New York: Penguin Books, 2002), 31-32.

3. Ron Hansen, *Mariette in Ecstasy: A Novel* (New York: HarperCollins, 1992), 167-68.

4. V. Sackville-West, *The Eagle and the Dove: A Study in Contrasts—St. Teresa of Avila, St. Thérèse of Lisieux* (London: Michael Joseph, Ltd., 1943), 14.

5. St. John of the Cross, *The Collected Works of St. John of the Cross*, trans. Kieran Kavanaugh and Otilio Rodriquez (Washington, DC: ICS Publications, 1991), 469.

6. Julia Kristeva, *Tales of Love*, trans. Leon S. Roudiez (New York: Columbia University Press, 1987), 154.

7. See Julian of Norwich, *Revelations of Divine Love*, chapters 60–65 (various editions). This text is also known as the *Book of Showings* (Julian had a total of sixteen revelations that are recorded here).

Part 4

1. Benedicta Ward, S.L.G., trans., *The Sayings of the Desert Fathers* (Kalamazoo, MI: Cistercian Publications, 1984), 111. I have quietly changed one exclusive pronoun to an inclusive alternative.

CHAPTER 11

1. Nikos Kazantzakis, *Christ Recrucified*, trans. Jonathan Griffin (London, England: Faber & Faber, 1962), 22. This novel is titled *The Greek Passion* in U.S. editions.

2. Paul Elie, *The Life You Save May Be Your Own: An American Pilgrimage* (New York: Farrar, Straus, and Giroux, 2004), xi.

3. Christopher O'Mahony, ed., *St. Thérèse of Lisieux by Those Who Knew Her: Testimonies from the Process of Beatification* (Dublin: Veritas Publications, 1975), 24.

4. St. Thérèse of Lisieux, *The Autobiography of Saint Thérèse of Lisieux: The Story of a Soul*, trans. John Beevers (New York: Image Books/Doubleday, 2001), 2-3.

5. St. Teresa of Avila, *The Collected Works of St. Teresa of Avila, Vol. 1*, trans. Kieran Kavanaugh, O.C.D., and Otilio Rodriguez, O.C.D. (Washington, DC: Institute of Carmelite Studies, 1987), 55.

6. Teresa of Avila, quoted in Jill Haak Adels, *The Wisdom of the Saints* (New York: Oxford University Press, 1987), 171.

CHAPTER 13

1. Ron Miller, *The Hidden Gospel of Matthew: Annotated and Explained* (Woodstock, VT: SkyLight Paths Publishing, 2004), 56-57.

2. Thomas Merton, in a talk to monks at the Abbey of Gethsemani on the subject of William Faulkner's short story "The Bear." Recorded by Merton and distributed on cassette by Credence Cassettes, Kansas City, MO.

GLOSSARY

Anchorite, anchoress: One who has devoted him- or herself to a solitary life of spiritual practice. Usually consecrated by the local bishop to such a life, during the Middle Ages.

Assumption: Catholic doctrine formally adopted by Pope Pius XII in 1950 stating that the Virgin Mary did not experience death but was "assumed" into heaven. The Feast of the Assumption of Mary is celebrated on August 15.

Beatification: A formal declaration from the Holy See that a deceased person should be *venerated* for the righteous life he or she led. This is a necessary step prior to *canonization,* although not all those who are beatified are canonized. A person who has been beatified is called *Blessed.*

Blessed: Appropriate title for one who has been *beatified.*

Canonization: A formal declaration from the Holy See that a blessed (see *Beatification*), deceased person is a saint and that veneration of him or her is efficacious for all Christians. The pope makes this declaration only after receiving detailed reports from the *Congregation for the Causes of Saints;* hearing testimony of firsthand witnesses, if possible; attesting to the holiness of the candidate's life; and authenticating miracles (at least two) performed through the candidate's intercession.

Cenobite: A person (monk or nun) who lives in a religious community rather than as a solitary. Traditional vows taken include a commitment to stability—remaining in community, obeying the abbot or superior, and living in poverty, holding all things in common.

Communion of saints: All the faithful, both departed and on earth, held by grace in one community as the children of God. Without reference to canonization, all the faithful departed are saints who urge on those of us who are still living, and we who are alive pray to them for spiritual intercession and prayer.

Congregation for the Causes of Saints: Located in Rome, this ecclesiastical body is convened after a person's *beatification* in order to investigate the cause for sainthood.

Consecrated virgins: Quoting Catholic church law, women who are "consecrated to God, mystically espoused to Christ and dedicated to the service of the church." Distinct from nuns, who live as sisters in community under a mother superior, a woman who has committed herself to this ministry is consecrated by her bishop and may or may not (without obligation) work in ministry for a local diocese. In Oregon City, Oregon, the U.S. Association of Consecrated Virgins fields questions from anyone interested in pursuing this vocation. Approximately one hundred women are living the vocation in America today. The Catholic church has always put high value on "perpetual virginity" as a way of fully consecrating oneself to God and turning away from the world. At the same time, marriage is a sacrament of the church, and this seeming contradiction is not lost on many Catholics today.

Cults of the saints: Popular movements of support for the veneration of a saint.

Curia: The body of leaders and other ministers who assist the pope in governing the Catholic church.

Diocese: A geographic region of the church headed by a bishop.

Doctor of the church: A saint who is also given this additional title by the pope or the church in recognition of the person's special gifts for teaching the faith. Teresa of Avila was the first woman declared a doctor of the church, while Thérèse of Lisieux is the most recent.

222

Glossary

Feast day: A day set aside each year for liturgically honoring a saint. A saint's feast day is usually the day of his or her death, which is also the day of his or her new, or eternal, life.

Iconoclasm: Practice of destroying religious images and removing them from churches and devotional life, as ordered and sanctioned by both secular and religious leaders in the eighth, ninth, and sixteenth centuries.

Indulgence: Essential part of the Catholic sacrament of penance; a remission of the "temporal punishment" of sin, either partial or complete (plenary), as administered by the church and enabled through acts of penance, devotions, and various forms of good works. (These same sins may have been forgiven by the grace of God, who alone removes the *eternal* punishment of sin.)

Mariology: Study and teaching of the doctrines on the subject of the Blessed Virgin Mary. Marian is the adjective used to describe the qualities, features, and influences of the Virgin.

Novena: Special petitionary prayer modeled after the prayer of the disciples of Jesus who waited in the upper room for nine days after Christ's resurrection.

Patron saint: A saint who offers a special relationship to people of a particular city, region, country, church, occupation, or physical/spiritual need. This term is also used for a saint who is chosen or given to an individual at baptism.

Sacred Heart of Jesus: This term refers to the literal, physical heart of Jesus Christ, often pictured in popular Catholic devotion as enlarged and superimposed on images of the Savior, as well as to the qualities of his heart: gentleness, caring, unsurpassed love. Catholic attention to the emblem of the *Sacred Heart* is similar to Protestant focus on becoming more like Christ, although it is accompanied by iconography that is always arresting. Devotion to the *Sacred Heart* took root in the church in the seventeenth century in France as people like St. Francis de Sales combated the heresy of Jansenism, which argued against the humanity of Christ. This devotion is usually practiced through conscious sharing

223

in Christ's agony in prayer the night he was arrested; the devout will spend an hour in prayer from 11 PM until midnight on Thursday evening before receiving Communion on the first Friday of the month with this in mind. The following prayer, attributed to St. Bernard of Clairvaux, is found in many Catholic prayer books:

> How good and sweet it is, Jesus, to dwell in your heart! All my thoughts and affections will I sink in the Heart of Jesus, my Lord. I have found the Heart of my king, my brother, my friend, the Heart of my beloved Jesus. And now that I have found your Heart, which is also mine, dear Jesus, I will pray to you. Grant that my prayer may reach you, may find entrance to your Heart. Draw me to yourself. O Jesus, who is infinitely above all beauty and every charm, wash me clean from my defilement; wipe out even the smallest trace of sin. If you, who is all-pure, will purify me, I will be able to make my way into your Heart and dwell there all my life long. There I will learn to know your will, and find the grace to fulfill it. Amen.

Second Vatican Council: The most important ecumenical (meaning that it encompassed all rites, or expressions, of the Catholic church) council since late antiquity. Convened by Pope John XXIII in 1962, Vatican II called for dramatic liturgical reforms, new roles for the laity in worship and religious life, greater outreach to the poor, and ecumenical openness to people of other Christian denominations and other faiths.

Stigmata: From a Latin word meaning "marks," signifies the five wounds of Jesus from the torture of the crucifixion: one in each hand, one in each foot, and a pierce in the side. The same wounds have appeared inexplicably on the bodies of saints, sometimes accompanied by bleeding. Francis of Assisi was the first stigmatic; he went to great effort to hide his wounds from others.

Theotokos: Greek word and name for the Blessed Virgin Mary: "Mother of God."

Veneration: Both Catholic and Orthodox doctrines make a clear distinction between veneration, which is due to saints, and worship, which is due only to God. To venerate literally means "to honor."

224

Glossary

Vigil lights (candles): For millennia, burning candles—placed in small glass or ceramic cups for safety reasons—have represented prayer and devotion. The burning flame represents the fervor of the devoted and continues the "vigil" of prayer long after the devoted has gone from that place. The lighting of candles is a popular form of devotion in cathedral churches throughout the world; the candles are usually placed before images of saints or shrines or within side chapels set aside for devotion to a saint or saints.

FURTHER READING

The following books represent a very selective and idiosyncratic list. There are several thousand books currently available on the saints, in addition to thousands more that are out of print but can easily be found in libraries and secondhand bookstores. The following are my recommendations for further explorations of the saints from various and distinct perspectives.

- The quintessential medieval perspective: Jacobus de Voragine, *The Golden Legend: Readings on the Saints*, trans. William Granger Ryan, 2 vols (Princeton, NJ: Princeton University Press, 1995). After the Bible and perhaps *The Imitation of Christ*, this was the most read book of the late Middle Ages.

- An American perspective: John F. Fink, *American Saints: Five Centuries of Heroic Sanctity on the American Continents* (New York: Alba House, 2003).

- A British perspective: David Hugh Farmer, *Oxford Dictionary of Saints*, 5th ed. (New York: Oxford University Press, 2003).

- Most comprehensive (multivolume): Alban Butler, *Butler's Lives of the Saints: New Full Edition*, ed. Paul Burns, 12 vols. (Collegeville, MN: Liturgical Press, 1995–2000).

- Most comprehensive (single volume): Alban Butler, *Butler's Lives of the Saints: New Concise Edition*, ed. Paul Burns (Collegeville, MN: Liturgical Press, 2003). Also: John J. Delaney, *Dictionary of Saints*, 2nd ed. (New York: Doubleday, 2003). (Delaney's book also includes the most accessible and comprehensive calendars of saints, both Western, or Roman, and Eastern, or Byzantine.) Also: Richard P. McBrien, *Lives of the Saints: From Mary and St. Francis of Assisi to John XXIII and Mother Teresa* (New York: HarperCollins, 2003). (McBrien takes a more liberal approach, incorporating many saints outside the Catholic tradition.)

- For patron saints: Thomas J. Craughwell, *Saints for Every Occasion: 101 of Heaven's Most Powerful Patrons* (Charlotte, NC: Stampley, 2001).

- For devotional use: Robert Ellsberg, *All Saints: Daily Reflections on Saints, Prophets, and Witnesses for Our Time* (New York: Crossroad, 1997). *Butler's Lives of the Saints: New Concise Edition* also works well for devotional use and is better than Ellsberg's book if you are seeking a more traditional approach. Both books are organized with a saint per day.

- Most helpful for identifying symbols of the saints in art: Gaston Duchet-Suchaux and Michel Pastoureau, *The Bible and the Saints*, trans. David Radzinowicz Howell (New York: Flammarion, 1994).

- Focus on women: Kathleen Jones, *Women Saints: Lives of Faith and Courage* (Maryknoll, NY: Orbis, 1999).

- Lighthearted: Alice La Plante and Clare La Plante, *Heaven Help Us: The Worrier's Guide to the Patron Saints* (New York: Dell Publishing, 1999). Also: Glenway Wescott, A *Calendar of Saints for Unbelievers* (New York: Harper, 1933). (A modern paperback reprint is also available.) Wescott's book is not always accurate, but it is hilariously witty and sardonic. Here is a sample from August 12, on the subject of Clare of Assisi: "In her old age, when her convent was invaded by Saracens, she rose from her sick-bed, knelt on the threshold, and sang to them appropriate menaces against the heathen out of the Old Testament. It must have been an unearthly thing to see and hear; professional invaders though they were, the Saracens took fright and fled."

- Most loved by pre–Vatican II Catholics when they were children (and still fun reads today): Joan Windham, *Six O'Clock Saints*

(1934); *More Saints for Six O'Clock* (1935); *New Six O'Clock Saints* (1945); *Here Are Your Saints* (1948); *Saints upon a Time* (1956) (New York: Sheed & Ward). Look for them in used bookstores. Here is a sample from *Six O'Clock Saints:* "Once upon a time there was a little girl called Teresa and she lived in the town of Avila in Spain. She was seven years old and her Favourite Thing to Do was reading, and whenever she read about anything she always wanted to go and do it herself."

INDEX OF NAMES

231

INDEX OF SUBJECTS

235

Books

Pg. True Devotion to Mary (1842 pub.) (
58   by Louis-Marie Grignion de Montfort
            SJ,

Imitation of Christ - by Thomas a Kempis
     (pub. 1418)

About Paraclete Press
Who We Are
Paraclete Press is an ecumenical publisher of books and recordings on Christian spirituality. Our publishing represents a full expression of Christian belief and practice—from Catholic to Evangelical, from Protestant to Orthodox.

Paraclete Press is the publishing arm of the Community of Jesus, an ecumenical monastic community in the Benedictine tradition. As such, we are uniquely positioned in the marketplace without connection to a large corporation and with informal relationships to many branches and denominations of faith.

We like it best when people buy our books from booksellers, our partners in successfully reaching as wide an audience as possible.

What We Are Doing
Books
Paraclete Press publishes books that show the richness and depth of what it means to be Christian. Although Benedictine spirituality is at the heart of all that we do, we publish books that reflect the Christian experience across many cultures, time periods, and houses of worship.

We publish books that nourish the vibrant life of the church and its people—books about spiritual practice, formation, history, ideas, and customs.

We have several different series of books within Paraclete Press, including the bestselling Living Library series of modernized classic texts; *A Voice from the Monastery*—giving voice to men and women monastics about what it means to live a spiritual life today; award-winning literary faith fiction; and books that explore Judaism and Islam and discover how these faiths inform Christian thought and practice.

Recordings
From Gregorian chant to contemporary American choral works, our music recordings celebrate the richness of sacred choral music through the centuries. Paraclete is proud to distribute the recordings of the internationally acclaimed choir Gloriæ Dei Cantores, who have been praised for their "rapt and fathomless spiritual intensity" by *American Record Guide*, and the Gloriæ Dei Cantores Schola, which specializes in the study and performance of Gregorian chant. Paraclete is also the exclusive North American distributor of the Monastic Choir of St. Peter's Abbey in Solesmes, France, long considered to be a leading authority on Gregorian chant performance.

Learn more about us at our Web site,
www.paracletepress.com
or call us toll-free at
1-800-451-5006.

Also by Jon M. Sweeney

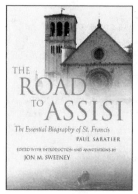

The Road to Assisi
The Essential Biography of St. Francis
Paul Sabatier
Edited with Introduction
and Annotations by
Jon M. Sweeney

*A Selection of:
Book of the Month Club
History Book Club
Crossings Book Club
The Literary Guild*

204 pages
ISBN: 1-55725-401-X
$14.95, Trade Paper

In his 1894 biography, Sabatier, a French Protestant, portrayed a fully human Francis, with insecurities and fear, but also a gentle mystic and passionate reformer who desired to live as Jesus taught his disciples. This modern edition features maps and illustrations, helpful side-bars, explanatory notes, and a complete bibliography.

"Sweeney achieves a fine balance between excellent scholarship and sweet accessibility for every average reader. To learn the life of Francis, to learn to love that life, and at the same time to experience the time in which he lived, this is the book to read." —Walter Wangerin, Jr., author of *St. Julian* and *The Book of God*

The St. Francis Prayer Book
Jon M. Sweeney

144 pages
ISBN: 1-55725-352-8
$13.95, Trade Paper

Kindle your prayer life with the words, guidance, and spirit of Francis of Assisi. This warm-hearted little book is a window into the soul of St. Francis, one of the most passionate, and inspiring followers of Jesus.

"An accessible, practical introduction to Franciscan prayer."
—*Publishers Weekly*

Available from most booksellers or through Paraclete Press:
www.paracletepress.com
1-800-451-5006. Try your local bookstore first.